# The Journal
## of
# Thomas Jefferson's Life and Times

Volume 1 ~ Number 2     Jefferson's "Academical Village"

**THOMAS JEFFERSON**
Heritage Society

Dedicated to preserving knowledge o f the life and times of the man who wrote the *Declaration of Independence* and the history of the nation formed on its principles.

# The Journal of Thomas Jefferson's Life and Times

**Managing Editor**
Professor M. Andrew Holowchak, *Philosophy, University of Colorado, Colorado Springs, Colorado*

**Editorial Advisory Board**

Professsor James Carpenter, Emeritus, *Bartle Professor, Graduate School of Education, Binghamton University, State University of New York, Binghamton, New York*

Richard E. Dixon, Esq., *Chairman of the Board, Thomas Jefferson Heritage Society, Clifton, Virginia*

Professor Brian Dotts, *Associate Professor, Department of Educational Theory and Practice, University of Georgia, Athens, Georgia*

J. David Gowdy, Esq., *Director, Washington-Jefferson-Madison Institute, Dallas, Texas*

Professor Arthur Scherr, *Assistant Professor of History, The City University of New York, Brooklyn, New York*

Professor Garret Ward Sheldon, *John Morton Beaty Professor of Politics, University of Virginia, Wise, Wise, Virginia*

Mr. James C. Thompson, II, *Publisher, Commonwealth Books of Virginia, Richmond, Virginia*

Mr. Tony Williams, *Senior Teaching Fellow, Bill of Rights Institute, Williamsburg, Virginia*

Professor Richard Guy Wilson, *Commonwealth Professor of Architectural History, University of Virginia, Charlottesville, Virginia*

Professor William Wilson, Emeritus, *Religious Studies, University of Virginia, Charlottesville, Virginia*

---

*Photo facing page:* Bust of Thomas Jefferson by Jean-Antoine Houdon (1789), © Collection of the New York Historical Society, USA/The Bridgeman Art Library

---

*The Journal of Thomas Jefferson's Life and Times* is published twice a year by the Thomas Jefferson Heritage Society as an imprint of Commonwealth Books of Virginia. www.tjheritage.org.

© 2017 by the Thomas Jefferson Heritage Society and Commonwealth Books of Virginia. All rights reserved. No part of this journal may be used or reproduced in any manner whatsoever without written permission. Printed in the United States of America.

ISBN (Paperback): 978-1-943642-48-9; ISBN (Ebook - EPUB): 978-1-943642-49-6

# Introduction

M. Andrew Holowchak, Ph.D.

What would become the University of Virginia was begun on October 6, 1817—200 years ago—as construction of Pavilion VII had started. Three presidents—Virginians Thomas Jefferson, James Madison, and James Monroe—were present. Eight years later, the first students of the university would attend classes.

More than any president, Thomas Jefferson did much to change the educational landscape in his day. His political philosophy, grounded on republican sentiments that were both liberal and communitarian, mandated systemic educative reforms—general education for the citizenry and higher education for the intellectual and moral elite. Unable to get off the ground his program for elementary schools, Jefferson turned attention to establishing a top-tier institution that would become in Charlottesville the University of Virginia.

This edition of *The Journal of Thomas Jefferson's Life and Times* is devoted appropriately to celebrating the 200th anniversary of the University of Virginia. The feature essay, "Thomas Jefferson's 'Academical Village,'" is by UVa's own Richard Guy Wilson—the world's foremost historian on Thomas Jefferson as architect. Architects and architectural historians Mark Wenger and Carl Lounsbury offer critical replies.

There follow eight shorter essays related to Jefferson's views on education and on the University of Virginia. James Carpenter writes of how Jefferson's "republican vision" shaped his educational views. Blanche Brick talks of how Jefferson's conception of natural rights led to a notion of equality of opportunity in education. Next, Richard Dixon shows how Jefferson's training in law helped shape the School of Law at UVa. There follows an essay, by White McKenzie Wallenborn, on Jefferson, medicine and the School of Medicine at UVa. I then contribute an essay on elite-level education and what I dub "the paradox of public service." Maurice Apprey then shares his thoughts on the experiences of black students early in the University of Virginia and how they were vehicles of "catalytic change." The eighth essay, by William Wilson, concerns how Jefferson's rebelliousness helped to shape the University of Virginia. The final essay, by Garrett Ward Sheldon, is an analysis of Jefferson's view of academic freedom and abuses of that concept today in higher education.

Jefferson hoped that the University of Virginia—molding tomorrow's leading politicians and scientists—would be the foremost elite-level institution in the country. While it has failed to achieve that ranking, it is generally recognized to be among the best. It currently ranks 25th among National Universities. Its Curry School of Education, Darden Graduate School of Business Administration, School of Engineering and Applied Science, School of Law, and School of Medicine are all highly ranked.

Moreover, there is Jefferson's architectural legacy: the *Pi*-shaped architectural masterpiece around The Lawn. With the help of William Thornton and Benjamin Latrobe, Jefferson drew up 10 pavilions, each singular in neo-Classical design, with adjoining dormitories, and the Rotunda at the north end. The overall design has gained recognition in 1987 by UNESCO as one of the world's most culturally significant landmarks.

## About the Contributors

**Maurice Apprey** is Professor of Psychiatry and the Dean of African-American Affairs at the University of Virginia. A psychoanalyst for children, adolescents and adults, he was trained at the Anna Freud Centre, London, and the Contemporary Freudian Society, Washington, D.C. He is the English language translator from French of Georges Politzer's *Critique of the Foundations of Psychology: the Psychology of Psychoanalysis* and coauthor of *Intersubjectivity, Projective Identification and Otherness*. He is co-editor with Shelli M. Poe of *Key to the Door: Experiences of Early African American Students at the University of Virginia*.

**Blanche Brick** has an M.A. in Education from George Washington University, an M.A. in History from the University of Hawaii and a Ph.D. in Education from Texas A&M University. Her graduate research was in the History of Education, where she specialized in the Changing Concepts of Equal Educational Opportunity as represented in the works of Thomas Jefferson, Horace Mann, and John Dewey. She retired in 2017 as Professor of History at Blinn College in Bryan, Texas, where she also served as Division Chair of Social Sciences.

**James Carpenter** was coordinator of the Doctoral Program in Educational Theory and Practice for the Graduate School of Education at Binghamton University, Binghamton, New York, where he was also an Associate Professor and coordinator of Adolescent Social Studies Education programs. One of the preeminent scholars on Jefferson and education, his research has focused on citizenship education and democratic education. His publications include "Jefferson's Views on Education:Implications for Today's Social Studies," "'The Development of a More Intelligent Citizenship': John Dewey and the Social Studies," and "Teaching All Students to be Leaders: The Forgotten Civic Skill."

**Richard E. Dixon** is the author of "The Case against Thomas Jefferson," in *The Jefferson-Hemings Myth: An American Travesty*, "Thomas Jefferson: A Lawyer's Path to a Legal

Philosophy," in *Thomas Jefferson and Philosophy: Essays on the Philosophical Cast of Jefferson's Writings,* and *The Virginia Presidents: A Travel and History Guide.* He is currently president of the Thomas Jefferson Heritage Society.

**M. Andrew Holowchak**—philosopher, historian, and editor of this journal—teaches philosophy at University of Colorado, Colorado Springs. He is author/editor of eight books and over 60 published essays on Thomas Jefferson and is acknowledged to be one of the world's foremost authorities on the thinking of Thomas Jefferson.

**Garrett Ward Sheldon** is John Morton Beaty Professor of Politics at The University of Virginia College at Wise, where he teaches Political Theory (Classics), Constitutional Law, and Religion and Politics. He is the author of several books and articles on Jefferson, including *The Political Philosophy of Thomas Jefferson* (Johns Hopkins University Press) and has been a Visiting Scholar at Oxford University; the University of Vienna, Austria; and Trinity College, Dublin, Ireland. Sheldon has received The Outstanding Faculty in Virginia Award, the highest honor conferred on an academic by the Commonwealth.

**Richard Guy Wilson** holds the Commonwealth Professor's Chair in Architectural History at the University of Virginia. A frequent lecturer and a television commentator, he has also published widely with many articles and books on different aspects of American and modern architecture and design, including *The American Renaissance* (1979), *McKim, Mead & White, Architects* (1982), *The AIA Gold Medal* (1983), *Machine Age in America* (1986), *Thomas Jefferson's "Academical Village"* (1993 and 2009), *Campus Guide: University of Virginia* (1999), *The Colonial Revival House* (2004), and *Harbor Hill: Portrait of a House* (2008), and "Thomas Jefferson's Architectural and Landscape Aesthetics: Sources and Meaning."

**William Wilson** is Professor Emeritus at the University of Virginia where for over three decades he offered courses in Philosophical Theology and Religion and Literature. He also served as Academic Dean for the undergraduate honors program (Echols Scholars) and directed the Graduate Fellowship at the Jefferson Scholars Foundation.

# Contents

**Feature Essay**

11  *Richard Guy Wilson:* Inspirational Learning: The Architecture of the University of Virginia

**Reply to Wilson**

23  *Mark R. Wenger:* Reply to Richard Guy Wilson

27  *Carl Lounsbury:* Thomas Jefferson's Architectural Legacy, A Reply to Richard Wilson

**Essays**

31  *James J. Carpenter:* Jefferson's Republican Vision and Citizen Education

39  *Blanche Brick:* Thomas Jefferson and the Natural-Rights Conception of Equal Educational Opportunity

47  *Richard E. Dixon:* Mr. Jefferson's Law School

61  *White Mckenzie Wallenborn:* Thomas Jefferson, Medicine, and the University of Virginia

71  *M. Andrew Holowchak:* Self and Selflessness: Elite-Level Education and the Paradox of Public Service in a Jeffersonian Republic

79  *Maurice Apprey:* Effective History: The Horizon for Sustained and Catalytic Change at the University of Virginia

85  *William Wilson:* Thomas Jefferson: University Founder and Virginia Rebel

93  *Garrett Ward Sheldon:* Thomas Jefferson's Conception of "Academic Freedom" and Its Current Condition in American Higher Education

101  *Book Reviews*

105  *Letter to the Editor*

# Inspirational Learning
# The Architecture of the University of Virginia

Richard Guy Wilson

THE OVERWHELMING, ONE MIGHT EVEN SAY, awe-inspiring experience of the University of Virginia takes place on many levels: the communal and the personal, the visual and the material, and the educational and the emotional. From a distance as one approaches what is called "The Grounds," a large circular brick structure with a curved dome captures the eye. One rarely encounters domes in the United States except for state capitals, a few courthouses, city halls, and now and then a religious structure or an old bank. The University's domed icon named the "Rotunda" has a huge classical portico with Corinthian columns and a massive triangular pediment. Proceeding further, a visitor enters the central space known as "The Lawn" of the University. Lying under your feet, the green grass of gently sloping terraces contrasts with the sky, arching overhead, and rows of white classical columns march out on both sides to amplify one's sense of being in a very special place. The long rows of columns are interrupted by large temple-fronted structures, sometimes crowned with a pediment, which are called "pavilions." The rows of columns on each side front a covered walkway that allows shelter but also creates a stunning effect when the sun hits the columns and creates lines of shadows on the brick pavement under your feet. Doors in the walkway give access to student rooms. The dramatic effect of the Classical columns is further enhanced by the trees that line each side of The Lawn and create another juxtaposition: the order of nature confronting that of man. Beyond the central space, the architectural drama continues with the curving single-brick walls which enclose gardens behind the large pavilions. Then on either side, one encounters another row of buildings called "The Ranges." Instead of columns, the covered walkway is articulated by semi-curved arches which provide another very different, yet mystifying spatial experience.

The story of the design and construction of the University has many elements and covers many decades. Thomas Jefferson began making drawings for the University in 1814, though his ideas for designing educational buildings began much earlier. Construction began in 1817 and the University was completed, except for a few details, by his death in 1826. Jefferson also drew up the list of books for the library, and devised the curriculum and the first class began in 1825. As a "university," the institution taught many subjects—

including the sciences, humanities, and languages—but also its students were expected to learn from the environment, that is, the buildings and the Classical architecture.

The University of Virginia in many ways represents the culmination of Jefferson's avid architectural interests that consumed him much of his life. A lady friend who knew and visited him in both Washington, D.C., and Virginia recorded his claim: "Architecture is my delight, and putting up and pulling down one of my favorite amusements."[1] He loved architecture and had one of the largest architectural libraries, if not the largest architectural library, in the young United States with more than 40 titles by authors such as Palladio, Gibbs, and others. Those were very expensive books and most were purchased from European dealers, since the first architectural book published in the United States was not until 1798, and only a few followed in the next 30 years.

Jefferson's architectural interests were wide-ranging. In addition to his Monticello—which he built, rebuilt, and remodeled almost his entire life, or from 1768 (Jefferson was born in 1743) to his death—he also designed and built an octagonal retreat at Bedford, Virginia (outside of Lynchburg), named Poplar Forest. His designs for these houses included not just the dwelling, but the landscape and gardens, the outbuildings, and also the interiors, and even the furniture.

Jefferson challenged the notion, prevalent in America, that designing buildings was simply about creating shelter. As the Marquis de Chastellux, in his *Travels in North America*, wrote, "We may safely aver, that Mr. Jefferson is the first American who has consulted the fine arts to know how he sold shelter himself from the weather." For him, architecture was something much broader. It included the exterior—its placement or site, the grounds, landscaping and gardens—as well as and especially the interior—the rooms or spaces, and also their furnishings, the drapes, color, and chairs. Additionally he advised many of his friends, e.g., James Madison and others, on the design of their houses, worked extensively on the planning of Washington, D.C., and drew up his own plans for the city—the President's House (the Executive Mansion, now the White House) and the Capitol. Other public buildings by him included the Episcopal church in Charlottesville, several courthouses for Virginia, the Virginia State Capitol in Richmond, and several other buildings.

Based upon a Roman temple, the Maison Carrée in Nimes, France, dating to c. 4 A.D., the Virginia Capitol is perhaps his most important architectural contribution, since it was the first public building in the young America republic and it helped set in motion an American architectural vision that looked back to Classical antiquity. His intentions for the Virginia

---

[1] This statement is attributed to Jefferson in Margaret Bayard Smith, *A Winter in Washington* (New York: E. Bliss and E. White, 1824) vol. 2: 261.

Capitol's design were very educational. As he wrote from Paris to James Madison (20 Sept. 1785), who served as one of the members of the legislative committee overseeing the new capital back in Virginia, "But how is a taste in the beautiful art to be formed in our countrymen, unless we avail ourselves of every occasion when public buildings are to be erected, of presenting to them models for their study and imitation?" Jefferson went on and claimed that the "the Masionquarree [sic] of Nismes [sic], one of the most beautiful, if not the most beautiful & precious morsel of architecture left us by antiquity.... It is noble beyond expression, and would have done honour to our country as presenting to travelers a morsel of taste in our infancy promising much for our mature age."[2] For Jefferson, architecture conveyed messages and, when done right, spoke to us—viz., became a vehicle for learning.

Jefferson spent five years (1784-1789) in Europe, principally in Paris, where he served as the American minister (today ambassador) to the Court of Louis XVI. He also traveled extensively and constantly observed and recorded what he saw—how crops were raised, the new machines, the landscapes, the gardens (which he loved and visited often), and of course architecture—with the aim of importing anything of value to America. His many letters convey his passion for architectural study, as when he writes in 1787 to Madame de Tesse (Mar. 20) that he is "violently smitten with the Hotel de Salm" in Paris and how he goes "daily to look at it." While in the south of France, he describes himself as "gazing whole hours at the Maison quarrée, like a lover at his mistress."

The next year Jefferson expresses concern that Americans traveling in Europe might not understand what they see, and thus, he offers some advice, or in his own words "hints," to the young American travelers, Rutledge and Shippen. First, he advises that they buy a plan of the town they are visiting and a book "noting its curiosities." Then the two are to walk around the town and its ramparts and "go to the top of steeple to have a view of the town and its environs." Concerning whether something is worth seeing, or not, he says, "Recollect that you will never again be so near it, that you may repent the not having seen it, but can never repent having seen it." Jefferson, always the advice-giver, tells Rutledge and Shippen to pay especial attention to "architecture worth great attention," much more so than painting and statuary which are "worth seeing but not studying." Instead, architecture "is among the most important arts and it is desirable to introduce taste into an art which shews so much."[3] The preference for architecture to painting and statuary is on account of its serviceability.

---

[2] See also, Fiske Kimball, *The Capital of Virginia*, eds. Jon Kukla with Martha C. Vick and Sarah Shields Driggs (Richmond: Library of Virginia, [1915] 2002); and Mark R. Wenger, "Thomas Jefferson and the Virginia State Capital," *Virginia Magazine of History and Biography*, vol. 101, 1993, 77–102.

[3] Jefferson, "Hints to Americans Traveling in Europe" 19 June 1788, eds. Wilson and Stanton, *Jefferson Abroad*, 249-51.

The reason for Jefferson's interest, or perhaps more appropriately his obsession, with architecture existed on several levels: personal and public. He liked to live well and designed and built houses that fulfilled his needs and also displayed his worth, intelligence, and status: our dwellings were mirrors of ourselves, as they expressed our values. Architecture—whether a courthouse, church, a school, or a state house—also had a public value, and their design and appearance conveyed meanings. He expressed his architectural values in Notes on the State of Virginia, which he largely wrote in the early 1780s, prior to his European venture. Notes on the State of Virginia was privately published in Paris in 1785, and then appeared in a commercial edition in London in 1787, and subsequently in many other editions. While as the title indicates the book is supposedly about Virginia, in actuality the canvas is larger and he references many other locations. The young nation was architecturally a disaster. "The genius of architecture seems to have shed its maledictions over this land."

In particular, Jefferson bemoans the poor quality of most dwellings and that they are built of wood. Wooden structures will need to be replaced every 50 or so years. Brick and masonry are far preferable and long lasting.

Jefferson also directs much criticism at the public buildings located in Williamsburg (which had been the Colonial and then State Capital until under Jefferson's governorship while it moved to Richmond in 1779). He gives very scant praise to the old state house and governor's mansion, and condemns the other major structures such as the College of William and Mary and the hospital. He writes that they "are rude, misshapen piles, which, but that they have roofs, would be taken for brick-kilns." He adds, "There are no other public buildings but churches and courthouses, in which no attempts are made at elegance."

Jefferson also bemoans the lack of education, as "a workman could scarcely be found capable of drawing an order." There existed no models from which the builders could learn. "Architecture being one of the fine arts, and as such within the department of a professor of the college, perhaps a spark may fall on some young subjects of natural taste, kindle up their genius, and produce a reformation in this elegant and useful art."[4]

Clearly Jefferson wanted a reform not just in architecture, but also in education, and he proposed that the Commonwealth of Virginia take over the College of William and Mary from the Anglican (soon to be the Episcopal) Church and make it a public institution. That came to naught (in 1907 it became a state institution). The type of architectural education

---

[4] Thomas Jefferson, *Notes on the State of Virginia*, ed. by William Peden (Chapel Hill: University of North Carolina Press, 1954, 152-54.

that Jefferson contemplated was not what today is the common practice in obtaining an architectural degree, but something very different. The definition of "architect" in Jefferson's time was rather nebulous and could include a builder who did all the construction and also some design work.[5] Typically one learned how to build/design buildings through the apprentice system, in which you worked for and learned from a person who had also received the same education. Very important to being an architect were building skills and also access to architectural books and treatise such as Palladio's *Four Books* or Gibbs' *A Book of Architecture*, which displayed the different details, their proportional measurements, and in a few cases, the entire building. Most of the books, as noted earlier, were published abroad, and many of the details shown were based upon measurements of earlier buildings. The books were expensive and rare and consequently some individuals who called themselves "architect" made copy tracings of illustrated details found in the books and then applied them to the project on which they were working.[6] Large building projects, such as a church or courthouse, seldom were the result of a single individual but usually the product of the vestry or a building committee who actually made the decisions.

Anybody, in Jefferson's day, could call himself an architect. Professional registration of architects at the state level did not emerge until the 1880s. In 1865, the first American school of architecture was founded at the Massachusetts Institute of Technology in Boston, though earlier in New York there were a few attempts to teach architectural drawing, but they were minor. A few schools of architecture at the collegiate level existed abroad, the most important being the École des Beaux-Arts in Paris. England had no schools, but merely an apprentice system. Germany by the mid-nineteenth century had a few schools of architecture. The roots of the École went back to the seventeenth century and the design and construction of Versailles, but it was radically reformed in the late eighteenth century under Napoleon I and moved to Paris. To the École, beginning in the 1850s, there came some young Americans to study architecture, and from it, came the American architectural educational system which still continues today.

In addition to the architect/builder of the period from 1700 to 1860 discussed above, there also existed the label "gentleman" or "amateur" architect which is a label sometimes applied to Jefferson. A gentleman architect was usually a wealthy male, with social status, who had access to an architectural treatise or two and used them to draw up or design a

---

[5] Carl Lounsbury, *An Illustrated Glossary of Early Southern Architecture and Landscape* (Oxford: Oxford University Press, 1994), Lounsbury notes that architect meant "An individual engaged in the design and the supervision of construction of buildings and structures."
[6] Bryan Clark Green, *In Jefferson's Shadow: The Architecture of Thomas R. Blackburn* (New York: Virginia Historical Society and Princeton Architectural Press, 2006).

building, normally their house, and then turn it over to builders who did the construction. The gentleman architect existed in England and Jefferson visited the work of several such as Lord Burlington's Chiswick, which greatly influenced his Monticello. In the United States, some of the elite houses of Virginia, such as Carter's Grove and Westover, resulted from an owner's ideas and books.

In New England, Peter Harrison (1716-1775), a wealthy former ship's captain and trader, produced a number of designs in Newport, Rhode Island, in the 1750s and 1760s, such as a synagogue, a trading market, and other structures like the first full temple fronted building in the country—the Redwood Library. Harrison is sometimes called a "gentleman's architect" and also known as the "first American architect." While viewed as a designer, Harrison was certainly involved in overseeing aspects of the construction of his designs.[7] Jefferson saw Harrison's work in Newport from June 14 to 16, 1784, while traveling to Boston to sail to England.

Around 1800, there appears on the American scene a few individuals who might be called professional architects, since their design work can be easily identified and since they made portions of their livelihood from designing. They also were very involved in construction. One professional was Benjamin Henry Latrobe (1764-1820), who received his training in England as an apprentice under eminent designers and arrived in 1796 in Virginia and then made his way north to Philadelphia, where he designed numerous important buildings (including the first American Catholic cathedral in Baltimore) and then to Washington, D.C., where Jefferson, as President, put him in charge of the U.S. Capital in 1803. In Boston, Charles Bulfinch (1763-1844) learned architecture while traveling abroad during and after the Revolution (he visited Jefferson in Paris) and then returned to design many important structures such as the Massachusetts State House, churches, houses for the Boston elite, and finally in 1817 to take on the U.S. Capital and complete it. Dr. William Thornton (1759-1828)—known as a "cosmopolite," as he was a medical doctor, was well-traveled, and owned several architectural treatises—was the original architect of the U.S. Capital, as he won the competition in 1792. He went on to design numerous other buildings in the Washington area, and was a friend of Jefferson. All were designers, but they also were very involved in construction. They supervised construction of their buildings and also did engineering work.

Was Jefferson a gentleman or amateur architect? He has been so labeled and certainly he had the books and designed for himself one of the most elite dwellings in the colonies

---

[7] There are a number of books on Harrison. The best is still Carl Bridenbaugh, *Peter Harrison: First American Architect* (Chapel Hill: University of North Carolina Press, 1949).

and young republic. But also as noted, he designed a host of other buildings that ranged from the grand to the more humble. Most importantly, he was very involved in the construction process of buildings he designed, especially at Monticello, Poplar Forest, and the University of Virginia. He knew how to mold bricks and lay them up, cut wood, and also carve classical capitals. The amount of his architectural work would put most architects to shame. He was never paid for his architectural designs, which might label him as an amateur, but his work ranks with any professional.

Education of the people and in particular of Virginians was another of Jefferson's lifelong passions. Consider, for instance, a letter to George Washington (4 Jan. 1786), "our [sic] liberty can never be safe but in the hands of the people themselves, and that, too, of a people with a certain degree of instruction." A few years earlier, Governor Jefferson proposed to the legislature in 1779 a Bill for the More General Diffusion of Knowledge, in which the state or commonwealth of Virginia would educate the populace. He proposed a three-tier system or what today we would call, primary, secondary, and collegiate levels and the commonwealth would take over the College of William and Mary. In his proposal, Jefferson states that single large brick structures would house the schools at the different levels. The legislature failed to pass the bill but Jefferson gained a reputation as a major proponent of education and public support for it.

Always ready to provide advice, Jefferson over the years wrote numerous letters to individuals about their plans for education. Frequently in his letters architecture played a significant role. Consider an 1810 response to an inquiry from certain trustees of Tennessee about a college. Jefferson advised that each professor should have a "a small and separate lodge," with "a hall below for his class and two chambers above for himself … the whole these arranged around an open square of grass and trees, which would make it what it should be in fact, an Academical Village, instead of a large & common den of noise, of filth, & of fetid air. It would afford that quiet retirement so friendly to study."[8] A few years earlier Jefferson had written to a friend, L.W. Tazewell (5 Jan. 1805), in Virginia about a proposed college:

> The greatest danger will be over-building themselves, by attempting a large house in the beginning, sufficient to contain the whole institution. Large houses are always ugly, inconvenient, exposed to the accident of fire, and bad in cases of infection. A plain small house for the school and lodging of each professor is best. These connected by covered ways out of which the rooms of the students

---

[8] Jefferson to the Trustees for the Lottery of East Tennessee College, 6 May 1810, *Jefferson Papers*, L.C.

should open would be best. These may be built only as they shall be wanting. In fact a university should not be a house, but a village.

These directives about the design of a school, which back in the 1770s begins with a single large structure and becomes by the 1800s a village around an open square, reflect Jefferson's changing and evolving concepts and his own architectural experience and education.

Jefferson's education began with tutors at the family farm outside of Charlottesville and then in another family estate near Richmond, and finally at a small "Latin" school run by the Reverend James Maury in Albemarle County. As one of the elite, he entered the Anglican College of William and Mary in Williamsburg which was housed in a single large brick structure now known as the "Wren Building." Located in front were two smaller brick structures—one a house for the President and the other for the education of Native Americans. Life at the college consisted of rowdy behavior on the part of the 49 male students in his class with plenty of drinking, food fights, and raids against the townspeople, sometimes led by one of the priests on the faculty. Jefferson admitted that he took part in these activities during his first year, but in his second year he came under the influence of William Short, the school's only secular professor, who taught science, mathematics, and philosophy. In 1762, Jefferson left the William and Mary to study law with George Wythe in Williamsburg, but he remained close to Short with frequent letters until Short's death in 1775. While a student in Williamsburg, Jefferson bought from a dealer outside the gates his first architectural book, the title of which remains unknown. This set off his lifelong pursuit of books on architecture and in the next few years he purchased copies of the Leoni edition of Palladio as well as works by Gibbs and others.

Over the years Jefferson returned to and lived in Williamsburg while serving in the legislature and then as Governor. Hence, he knew the single large college building very well. From 1771 to 1772, Jefferson was asked by the British Crown Governor, Lord Dunmore, to design an addition to the Wren building. Never built because of the uproar around the surging revolution, his design was for a closed quadrangle, which he probably drew from Palladio. However, by the mid-1780s, he condemned, in *Notes on the State of Virginia,* the William and Mary structure as "a brick kiln."[9]

The evolution of Jefferson's ideas about the architecture of a college or university took many years and resulted from new experiences. Undoubtedly his living abroad was important, though his many letters and notes from the time make no mention of collegiate

---

[9] Thomas Jefferson, *Notes on the State of Virginia,* 152–54.

architecture. Scholars have suggested that he certainly saw universities on his various travels in France and Italy, and also England, when he visited Oxford on April 9, 1786. Hence, what he observed remains unclear, but he certainly viewed some of the various quadrangles that made up most colleges, and perhaps he saw in Oxford the Radcliffe Camera, a circular library with a dome designed by James Gibbs and erected between 1737 and 1748. In his various trips on the continent, he passed by other colleges which were frequently fashioned out of monasteries and convents and again saw the concept of housing around an open space.

And so, by the early nineteenth century, Jefferson's ideas for a college/university had changed from a single large building into a village with the faculty and students living around an open space. In 1814, a group of men including his nephew Peter Carr, and his son-in-law, Thomas Mann Randolph, had decided to create the Albemarle Academy and they asked Jefferson to join the group as a trustee. He accepted. Within a short time, he drew up a plan with nine pavilions for the instructors interspersed with rooms for the students surrounded on three sides a large central space, and connected by covered walkways. On the reverse of his ground plan, Jefferson showed his idea for the front of the various pavilions for the professors on the Lawn with an elevation of it and also the connecting student rooms, the covered walkway and plans for them. Thus, Jefferson's ideas finally appeared on paper!

The idea of an academy located in Albemarle County caught on and in the next several years Jefferson and those involved in the concept got the state legislature to pass a bill in February, 1816, creating Central College. A small amount of money was appropriated that came from the sale of glebe lands confiscated from the Episcopal Church, and other sources and funds owed the Commonwealth by the Federal government. In a letter to Governor Wilson Cary Nicholas (2 Apr. 1816), Jefferson outlined the didactic function of the architecture. He explained that the school would exhibit "models in architecture of the purest forms of antiquity, furnishing to the student examples of the precepts he will be taught in that art." Jefferson's educational intentions regarding architecture and stated in *Notes on the State of Virginia* were not for a professional school of building designers, but were meant to promote knowledge and appreciation of good design as part of students' education.

In the next several years, the design of Central College, renamed the University of Virginia by the state legislature in January, 1819, came together. Jefferson altered his original plan to fit on to the acreage purchased outside the town of Charlottesville. Because of the hilly terrain, he narrowed the open space and created terraces on which the buildings sat. He also turned to his architectural colleagues Dr. William Thornton and Benjamin Henry Latrobe. He needed advice, since he had just sold most of his library to the United States

Congress with the loss of its library and he had few architectural books. Yet being a bibliomaniac, he also purchased the architectural books he needed.

To William Thornton (9 May 1817), Jefferson explained the concept of the university and asked for some assistance with the pavilion fronts: "these pavilions as they will shew [sic] themselves above the dormitories, [should] be models of taste and good architecture, & of a variety of appearance, no two alike, so as to serve as specimens for the architectural lectures. will you set your imagination to work & sketch some designs for us."[10]

Jefferson employed elements of Thornton's suggestion for the first pavilion to be erected, later named Pavilion VII. From Latrobe he got other ideas for fronts of the other pavilions and also the concept of placing a domed building at the center, which became known at the Rotunda. Thornton and Latrobe's involvement were central to the design of the University, but Jefferson was the person in charge and he altered their suggestions.

Jefferson employed two architectural treatises as the sources for the different facades. One was Leoni's *The Architecture of A. Palladio* which was in Jefferson's mind a modern. The other book used, Charles Errand and Roland Freart de Chambray's, *Parallele de l'Architecture Antique avec la Moderne* (1650) which delineated the ancient sources. From these books, he aimed to create a dialog, perhaps confrontational, between modern and ancient architecture. Pavilion I, located on the west side, is derived from the Doric design of Diocletian's Baths in Rome, as shown in Errand and Freart de Chambray, while across from it stands Pavilion II, which displays the Ionic design of the Temple of Fortuna Virilis in Rome as published in Palladio. A similar confrontation continues down the lawn, a modern across from an ancient, as with Pavilion VII, the Doric design of Palladio stands opposed to Pavilion VIII, the Corinthian design of Diocletian's Baths from Freart de Chambray. Thus, on the lawn at the University, the ancients and moderns are in dialogue, indicative of Jefferson's educational mission.

For the Rotunda, Jefferson took Latrobe's suggestion for a domed building and drew up a design based upon the Pantheon of Rome as shown in Palladio. As the head building for the university, it had chemistry labs and class rooms on the lower floors, and then he placed the library in the top floor, or dome room. Signifying the importance of the library Jefferson had the space ringed by the Composite order, which is the highest classical order, comprising volutes of the Ionic order capital with the acanthus leaves of the Corinthian order, and the only place on The Grounds that it appeared.

Jefferson explained several times that the reason for the differences on the pavilions on either side of the Lawn was that they were teaching tools. He writes to L. William Cabell Rives (25 Nov. 1825):

---

[10] See also TJ to Benjamin Latrobe, 12 June 1817.

The introduction of chaste models of the orders of architecture taken from the finest remains of antiquity, and of specimens of the choicest samples of each order was considered as a necessary foundation of instruction for the students in this art.... We therefore determined that each of the pavilions erected ... should present a distinct and different sample of the art ... the lecturer, in a circuit attended by his school, could explain to them successively these samples of the several orders, their varieties, peculiarities and accessory circumstances. Students should learn from their surroundings and know the differences of the orders and where they came from, whether the Baths of Diocletian or the Temple of Fortuna Virilis in Rome.

His intentions with architecture and with the university in particular lay with choosing the best models, which had received the approval of, or as he explained to James Buchanan and William Hay (26 Jan. 1786), "the suffrage of the whole world." The buildings he admired were perfect examples of cubic or spherical architecture irrespective of their political origins. Jefferson's choice of words indicates that he viewed the Maison Carrée and the Pantheon from a Burkian point of view: They had the approbation of the ages, and were models of natural law,[11] or as Jefferson had read in Lord Shaftsbury, "What is beautiful is harmonious and proportional; what is harmonious and proportionable is true, and what is at once both beautiful and true is of consequence agreeable and good."[12]

The story of the University of Virginia—or indeed of almost any building, especially those of Jefferson—is complicated. Every building—whether a dwelling, a state house or a university—has many reasons for existing, function and inspiration among them. Jefferson attempted to bring the best architecture to the American public and provide models for future Americans. He explains that to David Harding (20 Apr. 1824), when he gives his reason for choosing the Pantheon in Rome as the model for the University's Rotunda. "Antiquity has left us the finest models for imitation; and he who studies and imitates them most nearly, will nearest approach the perfection of the art." From the architecture of the University of Virginia, students would gain inspiration and insight, and hopefully carry their inspiration and insight to the wider world.

---

[11] Eleanor Davidson Berman, *Thomas Jefferson among the Arts: An Essay in Early American Esthetics* (New York: Philosophical Library, 1947), 124.
[12] Anthony Earl of Shaftsbury, *Characteristics of Men, Manners, Opinions, Times, Etc.*, ed. J.M. Robertson (London: Grant Richards, [1711] 1900), vol. 2, 268-69.

# Reply to Richard Guy Wilson

Mark R. Wenger

RICHARD WILSON MADE HIS ACADEMIC REPUTATION as a chronicler of the McKim, Mead and White firm, as a trusted interpreter of American Modernism, and as a student of American culture in the efflorescent years between Appomattox and the coming of the Great War. His work is deeply researched, intellectually substantial, and responsibly imaginative. In 1979, a heralded exhibit, American Renaissance 1876–1917, opened at the Brooklyn Museum of Art, highlighting his work on that important period.

In the years since, Wilson has turned his attention to Thomas Jefferson and his "academic village." Still the University of Virginia's spiritual core, this original compound remains largely intact, lying only a short distance from the rooms where "Mr. Wilson," has lectured and directed seminars over a period of forty years.

For a 1992 exhibition at the University's Bayley Museum, Thomas Jefferson's Academical Village: The Creation of an Architectural Masterpiece, Wilson edited an accompanying collection of three essays under the same title. The present essay is, in many respects, a distillation of that fine publication.

For the present essay, Wilson opens his narrative with a description of the Jefferson compound, explaining how visitors now experience it, spatially and visually. To provide context, he quickly outlines what is currently known of Jefferson's architectural career. That brief tour will be familiar to most readers of this journal, but it is useful to have the full sweep of Jefferson's activity before us as we consider his most ambitious architectural project—arguably the most consequential thing he completed.

Returning to the university, Wilson traces Jefferson's thoughts on education—and also the transformation of his cherished educational project from Albemarle Academy, to Central College, to University of Virginia. (Whatever the actual intent behind each of those succeeding names, their incremental expansion of the institution's geographic reach was as a masterly legislative gambit).

Jefferson's pronouncements on various aspects of architecture often appear anecdotally in scholarly writings about his projects. In the case of higher education, his brief, episodic comments do not constitute a systematic statement of belief, but they do serve to outline his conception of an ideal academic community, inspired by a powerful metaphor—the village. Wilson offers a complete record of these observations, and explains what he sees as a transformation and progressive elaboration of Jefferson's thought.

He suggests that Jefferson came to the "Academical Village" having abandoned an earlier, unitary conception, embodied in a single building. By Wilson's account, that first idea appeared in Jefferson's 1772 design for enlargement of the College of William and Mary, a scheme that would have produced a quadrangular enclosure, all under one roof.

One could argue that Jefferson was constrained, in this instance, by the extant building and by the fact that the he had supplied his design at the request of Virginia's royal governor, James Murray, 4th Earl of Dunmore. Was this William and Mary design really an unalloyed expression of Jefferson own mind on the matter? The immediate consideration driving this proposed enlargement of the College had been a reformation and expansion of the curriculum—projects very close to Jefferson's heart. Perhaps Wilson is correct, then.

Whatever Jefferson's original starting point, the important thing is his final, executed conception, arrived at after processing the suggestions of respected practitioners William Thornton and Benjamin Latrobe. For many years, that consultation clouded the importance of Jefferson's role as creator of the University. For this reason, the question of his standing as an architect is important Wilson affirms Jefferson in that title, suggesting, by implication, that the question of his "amateur" status is irrelevant. In this, he is correct. Jefferson involved himself intimately in the execution of numerous designs; he sometimes facilitated the process with large-scale details of important elements; his drawings for Monticello and other buildings frequently provided precise dimensioning and detailed notes on execution; on his own projects, Jefferson provided continuous, definitive direction on countless questions, and he frequently immersed himself in scheduling, procurement, and logistics. In every way that matters, Thomas Jefferson functioned as an architect.

As a consequence of his advancing age, Jefferson was less involved than he might have wished in the execution of his designs for the university. Not surprisingly, the physical realization of his grand scheme and its constituent parts required many on-site adjustments. These introduced relational subtleties between Jefferson's elements, enlivening what might otherwise have been a static design.

Perhaps Jefferson appreciated this problem. Admittedly, his varied designs for the Pavilions served an immediate, didactic purpose, about which he had been quite clear. But this diversity also embodied long-held theories concerning the nature of beauty—ideas Jefferson had surely imbibed. Writes philosopher Francis Hutcheson, "The Figures which excite in us the Ideas of Beauty, seem to be those in which there is *Uniformity amidst Variety* ... where the *Uniformity* of bodies is equal, the Beauty is as the *Variety;* and where the *Variety* is equal, the Beauty is as the *Uniformity*."[1] Perhaps this understanding of beauty, repeated frequently by later authors, could have reconciled Jefferson to the contingencies and variations bound up in an edifice embracing numerous distinct components, all constructed at different times, in varied order, by different individuals, each builder seeking to reconcile his own work to the land, and to other pieces already completed.

In laying out his view of the issues, Wilson is neither worshipful nor strident. He seeks only to know—and to communicate—bankable truths about his subject. Like Thomas Jefferson on another occasion, Wilson has delivered "the common sense of the subject, in terms so plain and firm as to command ... assent." Standing on that foundation, every reader is now free to decide what question comes next.

---

[1] Francis Hutcheson, *An Inquiry into the Original of Our Ideas of Beauty and Virtue,* 3rd ed., (London, 1729), 17.

# Thomas Jefferson's Architectural Legacy
## A Reply to Richard Wilson

Carl Lounsbury

WHEN ARCHITECTURAL SCHOLAR, FISKE KIMBALL published his catalogue of Thomas Jefferson's drawings in 1916, he began the process of resuscitating the third president's reputation as one of the most influential arbiters of architectural taste in the early American republic. At the beginning of the twentieth century, Jefferson scarcely figured in the scholarly and professional narratives about building; his contributions barely acknowledged or misplaced since so little was known about his skills as a designer or the precise roles he played in projects such as the Virginia State Capitol or the University of Virginia. Was he simply a gentleman architect who dabbled in design or an advocate who used his national prominence to sway opinion about public building in Washington and in his native state of Virginia? As Kimball sorted through the voluminous and disorganized collection of drawings that had languished for decades in the Massachusetts Historical Society, he discovered just how extensive and abiding Jefferson's interests were in architectural design beyond the hilltop confines of Monticello and came to appreciate a design philosophy that was formed from his close reading of the many architectural books that he had acquired. Jefferson once proclaimed that Andrea Palladio's *Four Books of Architecture* was his Bible and Kimball believed that he could read chapter and verse in the sketches and carefully rendered drawings scattered through hundreds of gridded sheets.

Kimball traced Jefferson's design aesthetic to the Renaissance rediscovery of the rules of ancient Roman architecture, which embodied the principles of balance, harmony, and symmetry. The fundamental units of design in classical architecture were the five distinctive orders, each one of which showed variations in the scale and decorative treatment of its column, base, shaft, capital, and entablature. Italian scholars and architects such as Palladio measured the remains of ancient Roman architecture and published their observations in books that circulated widely throughout Europe in the following centuries. These source books appealed to Jefferson whose enlightenment beliefs placed much credence in their codified rules of proportion and decoration. As a self-taught designer, he became a stickler for the correctness of classical details and was exasperated by the more relaxed rules of design practiced by contemporary craftsmen in America. Perhaps parading his pedantry, he chose to point out the shortcomings in the intercolumniation of the two-story pedimented portico of the second Capitol in Williamsburg in his *Notes on the State of Virginia*. He must have perplexed his own workmen at his retreat at Poplar Forest in Bedford County with the detailed instructions he sent them from the White House. He insisted on calling moldings by their classical rather than workbench names and specified the proportionate height of a surbase calculated precisely to the third decimal point. Country builders in backwoods Virginia used traditional language and shorthand methods and tools for establishing the size and shape of a chairboard. In so much of Jefferson's architectural design, there was the bookish ideal and the commonplace practices of members of the crafts trades who had to translate abstruse instructions into reality.

The University of Virginia was Jefferson's rejoinder to the slipshod and half-hearted embrace of classical architecture. Under his watchful eye, his compositions demonstrated the beauty and variety of classical forms when executed with greater precision. The buildings were indeed intended as models for public education. Yet the designs he and others devised were highly circumscribed, limited mainly to an ideal of classical Roman architecture that was already becoming outdated in the late 1810s. The European study of ancient architecture had been transformed dramatically in the late eighteenth century with the discovery and excavation of the ruins of Pompeii and Herculaneum, the drawing of the remains of Diocletian's Palace at Split, and the exploration of ancient Greek architecture in Sicily and the buildings on the Acropolis in Athens. Recording structures in these places revealed that ancient architecture was far more varied than what the Renaissance humanists had found in sixteenth-century Rome. Much of it defied the canonical rules laid out by Palladio and others two and three centuries earlier. Jefferson did acknowledge some of these newer interpretations of classical design at the University of Virginia where he introduced historical variations in the orders in the different pavilions, but these alternatives hardly embraced the new research that was summarized and translated into modern design by contemporary European architects, heralded in the United States by émigré architects such as Benjamin Henry Latrobe, who had a close working relationship with Jefferson even as he dismissed the limitations of the president's older perspective.

The backward-looking design aesthetic of Jefferson is evident in the details. Every original molding on the pavilions, the Rotunda, and the ranges in the academical village has a classical Roman profile, formed from the arc of a circle. By the late 1810s, carpenters and joiners who plied their trades outside of Charlottesville had given up their molding planes with their Roman ovolos and cymas for ones that were shaped to produce ancient Greek profiles, which were not based on circles but ovals. A subtle detail but one that heralded the displacement of traditional Roman forms with others that drew on different precedents.

Hundreds of Greek Revival temples built as courthouses, churches, academies, lyceums, and state capitols spread across America in the years immediately following the completion of buildings on the grounds of the University. Jefferson's Roman models did not proliferate outside Piedmont Virginia. Within half a century, the prestige and verities of classical design were challenged by a new aesthetic that valued the picturesque with it irregular massing and eclectic borrowing and blending of styles.

Richard Wilson is correct in locating the importance of Jefferson's architecture in the man's passion for creating models to promote the knowledge and appreciation of good design. The University of Virginia is a summation of that desire. In a rude landscape fraught with impermanent buildings, Jefferson wanted to elevate his countrymen's taste in building to his high standards, which he believed were based on true principals of design. This goal was essential for public buildings, which embodied this new democratic society's civic principles. His design for the new state Capitol in Richmond drew inspiration from an ancient Roman temple and the classical republican ideals associated with it. So too were the temple-fronted courthouses he devised for several Virginia counties. Public buildings needed to command admiration to bolster respect for the institutions housed in them. Yet, as he knew from his earliest years as a vestryman of an Anglican parish and as a justice of the Albemarle County court, the expense of building well sometimes provoked outcries of wastefulness and calls for simple, nondescript, but very practical models, sentiments that remain strongly embedded in debates about civic design. If few of his fellow citizens chose to emulate his models of Roman classicism, many did take up his advocacy for investing in praiseworthy civic architecture as scores of surviving antebellum public buildings testify. This belief in the efficacy of good design was perhaps Jefferson's most enduring architectural legacy.

# Jefferson's Republican Vision and Citizenship Education

## James J. Carpenter

GARRY WILLS DESCRIBED THOMAS JEFFERSON as an artist who spent his entire life "at state-craft *and* at visionary building." Jefferson's crowning architectural achievement, according to Wills, was the campus at the University of Virginia. The original complex of buildings "has an intricate unity" that can be experienced to this day.[1] However, as I argue in this essay, this intricate unity was applicable to more than an architectural community designed to promote learning in multiple and diverse fields of inquiry. It also represented the merger of Jefferson's vision for both republicanism in the United States and for an educational system to maintain and advance his idealized system of government. Each was grounded in a grassroots foundation that provided strength from the ground up.

## Jefferson's Republican Vision

Jefferson embraced republicanism not only as a safeguard against the corruptive practices of monarchies and rigid aristocracies but also as a means to individual and communal improvement. The American experiment, he believed, would be a model for the rest of the world to emulate. His faith in republicanism bordered on religious obsession. "The blessings of self-government," Jefferson wrote, exemplified "the sufficiency of human reason for the care of human affairs." Such an example, he hoped, would facilitate "spreading the happy influence of reason and liberty over the face of the earth."[2]

The ideal republic was more than a political system; it was a way of life to be lived at home as well as in the larger community. Historian Gordon Wood has argued that most eighteenth-century intellectuals, including the Founders, viewed the goal of a republic "by definition ... [as] the good of the people." The major challenge for a republican citizen was to understand and accept the necessity "to submerge his personal wants into the greater

---

[1] Garry Wills, *Mr. Jefferson's University* (Washington, D. C.: The National Geographic Society, 2002), 6-8.
[2] Thomas Jefferson, *Response to the Citizens of Albemarle*, ed. Merrill D. Peterson, Thomas Jefferson: Writings (New York, NY: Library of America, 1984), 491.

good of the whole." This was one of the core differences in the change of status from subject to citizen. To willingly "sacrifice his private interests for the good of the community" represented the essence of republican civic virtue in the eighteenth century.[3]

Jefferson clearly accepted this classic republican understanding. He was also very familiar with Enlightenment philosophy and was intellectually flexible enough to incorporate "both British liberal and classical republican qualities" into his own thinking. Jefferson found these qualities to be compatible and, as his personal philosophy evolved, each would dominate according to the historical circumstance. However, as Sheldon notes "both are present at all times."[4] Exercising republican virtue would also benefit the individual citizen. Writing to Peter Carr in 1785, for example, Jefferson advised encouragement "of all your virtuous dispositions, and exercise them whenever an opportunity arises." In doing so Carr would "derive the most sublime comforts in every moment of life, and in the moment of death" (19 Aug.1785). Jefferson believed that republican virtue started at home. As Gordon-Reed and Onuf argue, "The family ... would constitute the bedrock of republican society." Indeed, for Jefferson the source of republicanism, he told lawyer and author Samuel Kercheval, was located "not in our constitution certainly, but merely in the spirit of our people" (12 July 1816). This was a major distinction of republicanism from the hierarchical and more rigidly structured society of prerevolutionary Virginia where the planter elite dominated. After the Revolution, power, authority, and decision-making, republican enthusiasts believed, would be more diffused throughout all levels of society. Starting in the home, Jefferson believed, republican virtue "would radiate out to the community, the state, and the nation."[5] For example, Jefferson compared the "wretched" living conditions of "nineteen millions of people" living in France with the superior living conditions in the United States. The absence of "domestic bonds" led to a condition of "misery" that failed to produce "a happiness so temperate, so uniform, and so lasting" as that enjoyed by Americans. Their plight was the result of "one single curse, - that of a bad form of government" (TJ to Eliza House Trist, 18 Aug. 1785). Everyday household bliss in the United States was a byproduct of republicanism.

Jefferson also believed that property ownership would cause men to become immersed in local affairs. Indeed, he wrote to James Madison that "small landowners are the most precious part of a state" (28 Oct 1785). As such they had a greater stake in the decisions

---

[3] Gordon S. Wood, *The Creation of the American Republic, 1776-1787* (New York, NY: W. W. Norton & Company, 1972), 65 and 68. Wood's discussion of public virtue in a republic can be found in pages 65-70.
[4] Garrett Ward Sheldon, *The Political Philosophy of Thomas Jefferson* (Baltimore, MD: The Johns Hopkins University Press, 1991), 8, 17.
[5] Annette Gordon-Reed and Peter S. Onuf, *"Most Blessed of the Patriarchs:" Thomas Jefferson and the Empire of the Imagination* (New York, NY: Liveright Publishing Corporation, 2016), 11.

made by governments. Jefferson adhered to this belief throughout his lifetime. As he explained to Samuel Kercheval, "The true foundation of republican government is the equal right of every citizen, in his person and property, and in their management" (12 Jul 1816). And in the United States Jefferson believed this vested interest had proven that the people could be trusted to defend their interests and the rights of others. Jefferson found "the interposition of the people themselves on the side of government has had a great effect" and that they were "the best army" to defend against dangerous intrusions on their freedom (TJ to Edward Carrington, 16 Jan 1787).

Should we picture Jefferson's republicanism as a pyramid[6], the family would be the base. The people were crucial to successful republican government, and foundational to this power were the existence of good republican families. Families had civic functions to perform including fulfilling their civic duties to the community and preparing the next generation of republican citizens. A citizen's home "was also the elemental building block of the new republican edifice."[7] A virtuous father had the responsibility to instill republican virtues in his children.

Girls too needed to understand republicanism. Even though they were eventually excluded from Jefferson's formal educational proposals beyond elementary education, they needed to be able as mothers "to educate their own daughters, and even to direct the course for sons, should their fathers be lost, or incapable, or inattentive." Jefferson felt it obvious that girls learn skills of "house-hold economy" since "the order and economy of a house are as honorable to the mistress as those of the farm to the master" (TJ to Nathaniel Burwell, 14 Mar 1818). A good republican household was an efficient and orderly household.

The next tier consisted of the wards. The ward system for Jefferson was critical. A ward was a geographic area roughly five or six square miles in size. Each ward would function as a political unit responsible for providing the requisite services for its citizens such as education and police protection. For Jefferson, the wards would be analogous to the New England townships for which he had great respect. In fact, due to "narrow limits of space and population," he did not believe a pure republican government "would be practicable beyond the extent of a New England township" (TJ to John Taylor, 28 May 1816). Such local experiences served to create the necessary civic skills "by developing both their affectionate regard for the community and nation and their rational faculties requisite to wise public deliberation." Recognizing the fragile realities of American republicanism, Jefferson believed wards and towns were to be the foundation upon which each level of the

---

[6] M. Andrew Holowchak uses this metaphor in his *Thomas Jefferson's Philosophy of Education: A Utopian Dream* (New York, NY: Taylor and Francis, 2014).
[7] Gordon-Reed and Onuf, *"Most Blessed of Patriarchs,"* 174.

federal experiment would be built. If citizens were educated with the proper tools, "republican virtue might be safely extended to the increasingly centralized powers in county, state, and federal republics."[8] Wards and townships, he tells Kercheval, were "the wisest invention ever devised by the wit of man for the perfect exercise of self-government (12 Jul 1816)." Again using New England townships as examples, Jefferson felt that for larger issues of importance, citizens of each ward could meet on the same day "to produce the genuine sense of the people on any required point" (TJ to John Adams, 28 Oct. 1813).

The next levels of this pyramid would include counties, the state, and then the nation.

However, political power would be diffused with the ultimate authority residing with individual citizens and the wards. "It is by dividing and subdividing these republics from the great national one down through all its subordinations, until it ends in the administration of every man's farm by himself; by placing under every one what his own eye may superintend, that all will be done for the best" (TJ to Joseph C. Cabell, 2 Feb. 1816). Ever concerned with abuse of political power, Jefferson believed the "little republics [e.g. the wards] would be the main strength of the great one" (TJ to John Tyler, 26 May 1810). Political authority would thus rest with the people and popular control of the higher levels of government would serve as effective checks on them. Power would be diffused and would emanate from the grass roots up.

## Educating Republican Citizens

Like others of the founding generation, Jefferson believed that citizens needed to be taught their new roles and responsibilities in a republic. Among the founders, no one developed with more detail a complete educational system to prepare properly future generations of republicans, and no one advocated for it as vigorously as Jefferson did until his death in 1826. Not only did Jefferson propose a complete scheme for educating Virginians, but in doing so he also consistently incorporated his republican vision at every level of his plan. It is beyond the scope of this essay to assess if elements of his plan conflicted with his vison of republicanism. Yet what is clear is Jefferson's belief that educating future citizens was central to the survival and growth of the new republican government. General education, offered to each citizen, would give citizens much needed self-sufficiency though elementary education, focused on reading, writing, and basic math. Higher education, through an

---

[8] Garrett Ward Sheldon, *The Political Philosophy of Thomas Jefferson*, 144.

institution like the University of Virginia and the grammar schools would funnel some of the most promising citizens in genius and virtue from ward schools to a university.

Jefferson first submitted a bill detailing a complete educational system to the Virginia legislature in 1779 as part of a comprehensive reform package. He submitted a second, very similar plan in 1817.

Like his conception of republicanism, Jefferson's educational thinking can be represented as a pyramid. Each of his proposals consisted of three levels.

The first level consisted of the primary schools. These schools would be free to all white children (in his later plan only white boys were eligible) for three years "and as much longer, at their private expense, as their parents, guardians, or friends, shall think proper." Students would be given a firm foundation in "reading, writing, and common arithmetick" as well as reading important works in ancient Greek, Roman, English, and American history.

Each year one student "of the best and most promising genius and disposition" and who lacked the funds to further his education would be appointed to attend the next level in the scheme, the grammar school, at no expense. There were to be twenty of these schools, each to be centrally located to serve three or four counties for those boys who came from families with the means to attend. The curriculum of these schools included "the Latin and Greek languages, English grammar, geography, and the higher part of numerical arithmetick, to wit, vulgar and decimal fractions, and the extraction of the square and cube roots."[9] After a rigorous two year selection process, one exceptional state-supported student could continue his grammar-school education for four years. At the conclusion of their grammar-school education, students would essentially be divided into two distinct classes of citizens: "those destined for labor ... [and] their companions, destined to the pursuits of science." The former would "engage in the business of agriculture, or enter into apprenticeships" while the latter would "proceed to the college" (TJ to Peter Carr, 7 Sept. 1814).

Those proceeding to college would attend the apex of Jefferson's educational pyramid—in 1779, the College of William and Mary, and in 1817, the University of Virginia. In addition to those who could afford to attend, one outstanding student without the requisite funds would receive a three year state scholarship to attend. Students attending this level of education were again divided into two categories: "I, Those who are destined for learned professions, as means of livelihood; and 2, The wealthy, who, possessing independent

---

[9] Thomas Jefferson, *A Bill for the More General Diffusion of Knowledge*, ed. Merrill D. Peterson, *Thomas Jefferson: Writings*, 367-71.

fortunes, may aspire to share in conducting the affairs of the nation, or to live with usefulness and respect in the private ranks of live" (TJ to Peter Carr, 7 Sept. 1814). The extensive university curriculum, he writes in 1817, included "history and geography, ancient and modern; natural philosophy, agriculture, chemistry, and the theories of medicine, anatomy, zoology, botany, mineralogy and geology; mathematics, pure and mixed; military and naval science; ideology, ethics, the law of nature and of nations; law, municipal and foreign; the science of civil government and political economy; languages, belles lettres; and the fine arts generally."[10]

In each of his two educational proposals, Jefferson sought to provide all citizens with an initial education suitable to his own station in life, be it farmer or politician. Additionally, as I will describe below, a citizen's education was intricately connected to Jefferson's understanding of republicanism.

## Citizenship Education as a Reflection of Republicanism

Jefferson's faith in education as the best safeguard against government abuse is well known. As he wrote to lawyer and mentor George Wythe, "No other sure foundation can be devised, for the preservation of freedom and happiness" (13 Aug. 1786). But Jefferson felt that education also served individual citizens by preparing them to be good republicans at home and in their community, hence his reference to happiness above. A proper education enabled citizens "to form them[selves] to habits of reflection and correct action, rendering them examples of virtue to others, and of happiness within themselves."[11] Therefore, there was more than a casual relationship between his visions for both republicanism and education.

Structurally republicanism and education were integrally connected. Both visions were designed as pyramids and in each case wards were a critical feature. Jefferson envisioned a more intimate relationship for citizens in a republican government and the wards were the arenas in which all citizens regardless of class or status operated. They were "the bedrock and mainstay of his republican schema" and were "to be structured such as to provide for the happiness and independence of the citizens in them."[12]

---

[10] Thomas Jefferson, *A Bill for Establishing a System of Public Education,* in gilderlerhman.org/collections, accessed 30 June 2017.
[11] Thomas Jefferson, "Report of the Commissioners Appointed to Fix the Site of the University of Virginia," *Thomas Jefferson: Writings,* 460.
[12] M. Andrew Holowchak, "Individual Liberty and Political Unity in an Expanding Nation: The Axiological Primacy of Wards in Jefferson's Republican Schema," ed. M. Andrew Holowchak, *Thomas Jefferson and Philosophy: Essays on the Philosophical Cast of Jefferson's Writings* (Lanham, MD: Lexington Books, 2014), 52.

The wards were home to republican families and also responsible "for the small, and yet numerous and interesting concerns of the neighborhood." They would provide civic needs such as police protection, adjudication of local disputes, and schools. In these local political subdivisions, he tells Kercheval, "the whole is cemented by giving to every citizen, personally, a part in the administration of the public affairs" (12 July 1816). County, state, and national governments "would form a gradation of authorities, standing each on the basis of law, holding every one its delegated share of powers, and constituting truly a system of fundamental balances and checks for the government." Thus, as he writes to Cabell, "every man is a sharer in the direction of his ward-republic, or of some of the higher ones, and feels that he is a participator in the government of affairs, not merely at an election one day in the year, but every day" (2 Feb. 1816).

Likewise, Jefferson's educational pyramid was designed to reinforce the principles of republicanism in the mind of each citizen to "enable him to read, to judge & to vote understandingly on what is passing" (TJ to Littleton Waller Tazewell, 5 Jan. 1805). Here too wards offered local control for the elementary schools, which would "provide an education adapted to the years, to the capacity, and the condition of every one, and directed to their freedom and happiness." Indeed "the principal foundations of future order will be laid here."

Each level of schooling was designed to introduce and reinforce notions of classic republican values and virtue. For example, religious texts were not to be used at the elementary level because the students were "at an age when their judgments are not sufficiently matured for religious enquiries."[13] Similarly, at the university there would not be a professor of divinity "in conformity with the principles of our Constitution."[14]

Just as Jefferson's understanding of citizenship was grounded from the bottom up, so too did he envision schooling. The ward schools were controlled by the local constituents because "if it is believed that these elementary schools will be better managed by the governor and council, the commissioners of the literary fund, or any other general authority of the government, than by the parents within each ward, it is a belief against all experience" (TJ to Joseph C. Cabell, 2 Feb 1816). Overseers of the ward schools would select the site for the grammar schools as well as appointing "a visiter [sic] from each county." The "visiters" would then select supervisors for "the grammar schools in their respective counties." In this way, Jefferson indirectly linked the management of the grammar schools to the wards.

Moreover, even the university was meant to resemble a republican community. Structurally, it "should not be an house but a village" (TJ to Littleton Waller Tazewell, 5 Jan.

---

[13] Thomas Jefferson, *Notes on the State of Virginia*, ed. William Peden (New York, NY: W. W. Norton & Company, 1982), 147.

[14] Thomas Jefferson, *Report of the Commissioners Appointed to Fix the Site of the University of Virginia*, 467.

1805), and constructed in such a manner that it "would afford that quiet retirement so friendly to study." Each professor would assume an almost paternal role in supervising "the students adjacent to his lodge" including possibly sitting "at the head of their table." This familial and ward-like atmosphere would encourage students "to health, to study, to manners, morals, and order" (TJ to Messrs. Hugh L. White *et al.*, 5 May 1810). Products of this system would not only be able to protect themselves against potential threats to their liberties but would also be able to live their lives as virtuous republican citizens regardless of their socio-economic status.

Jefferson, therefore, believed republicanism was a way of life, meant to permeate all areas of daily experience. Education was the vehicle by which the principles of republicanism, expressed fully for instance in his First Inaugural Address, would be passed on from one generation to the next. Consequently, his plan for educating future Virginians to be good republican citizens reflected the same grassroots foundation as did his vision for good republican government.

The strength of any structure was a solid foundation, and for Jefferson, that strength started in the home and extended upward first through the wards and eventually to the state and national levels. Citizens would share in this sense of equal responsibility. Gordon-Reed and Onuf describe this as "recognizing the civic capacity—and kinship—of fellow citizens."[15] Regardless of social standing, economic status, or educational level, Jefferson's republicanism envisioned citizen equality guaranteed by a republican educational system.

---

[15] Gordon-Reed and Onuf, *"Most Blessed of Patriarchs,"* 317.

# Thomas Jefferson and the Natural-Rights Conception of Equal Educational Opportunity

Blanche Brick

WHEN JEFFERSON WROTE THAT "all men are created equal," it would seem that his views on natural rights and equality would have been clearly stated and settled. This was not the case, however. His words do not appear to be vague or obscure, yet few statements have been examined and explained more frequently by later generations of political historians

In *The Living Thoughts of Thomas Jefferson,* John Dewey wrote that for Jefferson, "The natural equality of all human beings was not psychological nor legal. It was intrinsically moral."[1] But attempts to put such a moral principle into practice have consistently led to debates about what public policy should be, and nowhere more glaringly than in the debates over the educational policy of a democratic country like the United States. Perhaps this is because, as Dewey went on to say, "the 'self-evident truths' about the equality of men by creation and the existence of 'inherent and inalienable rights,' appear today to have a legal rather than a moral meaning."[2]

That was not the case with Jefferson, however. There was no confusing moral equality and inalienable rights with each individual's natural rights. As Robert Heslep explained in Jefferson's view of equal educational opportunity based on his natural rights philosophy, "Education should aim to develop each student's faculties fully with respect to his happiness."[3]

For Jefferson, all were equal in their right to be unequal. As Merle Curti noted in *Human Nature in American Thought,* Jefferson realized that "superior powers of reasoning and of judgment were not confined to any one class, however wealthy and socially prominent."[4] Therefore, Jefferson's natural-rights philosophy of equal opportunity required one to ignore rather than to recognize family or class background.

---

[1] John Dewey, *The Living Thoughts of Thomas Jefferson* (Philadelphia: David McKay Company, 1940), 24.
[2] John Dewey, *The Living Thoughts of Thomas Jefferson,* 23.
[3] Robert D. Heslep, *Thomas Jefferson and Education* (New York: Random House, 1969), 89–90.
[4] Merle Curti, *Human Nature in American Thought* (Madison, Wisconsin: University of Wisconsin Press, 1980), 81.

In *Thomas Jefferson and Education,* Heslep stated, "Jefferson's principles of human nature, morality and political society are integral to his philosophical orientation to education."[5] He cautioned, however, that it was difficult to understand Jefferson's ideas because they were closely tied to his metaphysical ideas, which Heslep found to be somewhat obscure.

Did Jefferson have a clear and concise view of human nature, and if so, what did that view imply for his educational plans from elementary school through his "Academical Village"? These are the questions which this article will address.

In order to understand Jefferson's view of the nature of man, one must understand first what he meant by "man" and what he meant when he spoke of "inherent and inalienable rights." These terms reflected his religious view of how the universe was conceived, a view defined as deism in which "the world is a great machine operating according to natural laws, but God is its first cause and initiator."[6] As a deist, Jefferson accepted the idea of an ordered cosmos and, as Lee points out, "it followed, therefore, for Jefferson, that the nature of man was an essence, bestowed upon man as man by God at creation."[7]

While Jefferson used the term "man" to include humankind in the broadest meaning of that term when referring to the role of humans as related to a creator, he also distinguished between different categories of "man" when referring to specific roles of individuals by race, gender, and political rights.[8] And these distinctions are crucial in understanding his views on education that culminated in the creation of his "Academical Village" which did not include most men, as well as women, Blacks, or Indians. This article will focus on the view of human nature as it applied to "man" in Thomas Jefferson's eighteenth-century world, which at times applied to all mankind in the broadest sense of that word, but for the purposes of his educational plans for his "Academical Village," was primarily applied to those young men who would have the responsibilities of becoming lawyers, doctors, politicians, and men of science.

As one of the foremost American philosophers of the Enlightenment, Jefferson subscribed to the idea that natural laws did apply to all human beings and were discoverable by the use of the mind. Curti found this belief in the concept of natural law to be the core of the eighteenth-century thought. "The conviction that man's uniqueness was better understood by the use of natural faculties of the mind than by supernatural revelation and

---

[5] Roger D. Heslep, *Thomas Jefferson and Education,* 78.
[6] Freeman Butts, *A Cultural History of Western Education* (New York: McGraw-Hill, 1955), 282.
[7] Gordon C. Lee, *Crusade against Ignorance: Thomas Jefferson on Education* (New York: Columbia University Teachers College Press, 1961), 10-1.
[8] John B. Boles, *Jefferson: Architect of American Liberty* (New York: Basic Books, 2017), 2-3.

metaphysics."⁹ But, as Wills pointed out in Inventing America, Jefferson's view of the nature of man was based on a belief in innate endowments and a moral sense more than it was on the capacity of reason to arrive at moral truths. "Jefferson's moral sense ... is submitted in some measure to reason but is not itself an act of reason."¹⁰ Writing to his nephew, Peter Carr (10 Aug. 1787), Jefferson said: "The moral sense, or conscience, is as much a part of man as his leg or arm.... This sense is submitted, indeed, in some degree, to the guidance of reason; but it is a small stock which is required for this."

Garry Wills emphasized how central to an understanding of the philosophical ideas of the eighteenth century and to Jefferson's educational ideas is the prevailing concept of the innate moral sense of human nature. He writes, "Students of Jefferson's philosophy have known that he believed in the moral sense as a separate faculty, but they have underestimated the importance of that fact."¹¹

Most authorities on Jefferson agree that he was directly influenced by the philosophers of the Scottish Enlightenment, in particular Frances Hutcheson, Lord Kames, and Thomas Reid, who emphasized a universal innate moral sense. Hutcheson was very clear about the role of reason in the development of a moral sense in human nature. "Human nature was not left quite indifferent in the affair of virtue, to form to itself observations concerning the advantage or disadvantage of actions, accordingly to regulate its conduct."¹² Jefferson echoed this sentiment in a letter to John Adams (14 Oct. 1816) regarding the views of the French economist, Destutt de Tracy. "I gather from his other works that he adopts the principle of Hobbes, that justice is founded in contract solely, and does not result from the construction of man. I believe, on the contrary, that it is instinct, and innate, that the moral sense is as much a part of our constitution as that of feeling, seeing, or hearing."

This belief in the innate quality of the moral sense should not suggest, however, that Jefferson was not aware of the influence of the environment upon innate abilities. In arguing for an essential human nature, he recognized the need for an equal opportunity to develop these abilities. "At the very heart of his liberal theory was a confidence that man could improve himself through education."¹³

---

⁹ Merle Curti, *Human Nature in American Thought*, 71.
¹⁰ Garry Wills, *Inventing America: Jefferson's Declaration of Independence* (New York: Doubleday and Co., 1978), 202.
¹¹ Gary Wills, *Inventing America*, 199.
¹² Francis Hutcheson, quoted in Wills, *Inventing America*, 198–99 and 205.
¹³ Thomas E. Spencer, "Education and American Liberalism: A Comparison of the Views of Thomas Jefferson, Ralph Waldo Emerson and John Dewey," Ph.D. Dissertation, University of Illinois (Ann Arbor: University Microfilms International, 1963) 64.

In addition to the Scottish philosophers and the political philosophy of John Locke, he was also aware of and influenced by the French philosophers, particularly Helvetius and D'Holbach. As Curti pointed out, he expressed a high regard for Pierre Georges Cabanis' "Rapports du physique et du moral de l'homme," which viewed psychology in physiological terms completely divorced from metaphysics.[14]

This does not imply, however, that Jefferson was a behaviorist in any sense of the meaning now applied to that word. His belief in the innate moral sense of man left man a moral agent able to know good and responsible for choosing it or bearing the consequences of his choice. Human nature was based on fixed principles and endowed with a knowledge of being influenced by one's environmental conditions. Man was not viewed as hopelessly trapped by his human nature. Education could serve to direct and to develop the more favorable aspects while controlling the less desirable. Writes Jefferson: "We should be far... from the discouraging persuasion that man is fixed, by the law of his nature. ... Education engrafts a new man on the native stock, and improves what in his nature was vicious and perverse into qualities of virtue and social worth."[15]

As Dumas Malone observed that experiment and change were central to Jefferson's views, "His genius was not merely that of freedom and reasonableness. It was also the genius of experiment and change."[16] Lawrence Cremin saw this belief in change as integral to Jefferson's educational philosophy. "The entire scheme ... was founded upon the view that human nature was not fixed, that man was essentially improvable, and that education was the chief means of effecting that improvement."[17]

Nowhere in his writing is his attempt to reconcile the differences in his view of innate moral and intellectual ability with the influence of environmental conditions more visible than in his consideration of the plight of the slaves in America. In *Notes on the State of Virginia*, he voiced the suspicion that the poor showing Blacks made in reasoning power resulted from an innate rather that an environmental deficiency.[18]

Jefferson obviously struggled to reconcile his views regarding innate inheritance versus environmental influences and this struggle resulted in a complexity in his thought that has often been oversimplified. While he definitely considered the black slaves to be

---

[14] Merle Curti, Human Nature in American Thought, p. 81.
[15] Thomas Jefferson, "Report to the Commissioners Appointed to Fix the Site of the University of Virginia, 1 Aug. 1818," in Roy J. Honeywell, *The Educational Work of Thomas Jefferson* (Cambridge, Mass.: Harvard University Press, 1931), Appendix J, 251.
[16] Dumas Malone, *Jefferson and the Rights of Man* (Boston: Little, Brown, 1951), 179.
[17] Lawrence Cremin, American Education: *The National Experience 1783—1876* (New York: Harper & Row, 1980), 111.
[18] Thomas Jefferson, *Notes on the State of Virginia, The Life and Selected Writings of Thomas Jefferson*, eds. A. Koch & William Peden (New York: Random House, 1944), 257-58.

inferior to the white man, he also wrote that "though the black man, in his present state, might not be equal in body and mind to the white, it would be hazardous to affirm that, equally cultivated for a few generations, he might not become so."[19]

Jefferson's views on the education of women also reflected his view of their assigned roles in eighteenth-century society. He showed great concern in selecting proper educational arrangements for nine-year-old Patsy, his pet name for his eldest daughter Martha, in Philadelphia and Boston and later in Paris, when she accompanied him there in 1784. He also included girls in his Bill for the More General Diffusion of Knowledge which he presented to the Virginia legislature in 1779. He proposed to have the first three years of education include girls, along with young boys, provided at public expense. He did not, however, include girls among those from whom "the best genius would be selected and provided further education at public expense." As Cynthia Kierner points out in her book *Martha Jefferson Randolph, Daughter of Monticello,* his view of education reflected the role of women in society at that time.[20] Education that prepared one for a profession was not part of that view, though having educated wives and mothers was important because, as Jefferson noted in a letter to the marquis de Chastellux (7 June 1785), "The chance that in marriage she will draw a blockhead I calculate at about fourteen to one," leaving the education of her children to "rest on her own ideas and direction without assistance."

Given the necessity of very strictly defined rolls in the care of the young in his day and the fact that technology had not developed to the extent of allowing women to participate in the workforce as it would after the Civil War, his views on the education of women are actually more progressive than those of most men during his time period. Jefferson urged his daughters to read, though the reading lists he compiled for young men, such as his kinsmen Robert Skipwith and Peter Carr, were far more specific and varied than what he prescribed for his daughters, for whom he believed reading would be chiefly a weapon "against ennui" born of rural isolation and ultimately "useful only for filling up the chinks of more useful and healthy [domestic] occupations."[21] He did support girls receiving at least an education that would make them literate mothers and wives, and as Kierner points out, he valued the fact that his wife was not only literate but intellectually challenging as a companion, noting that he spent many happy hours reading *Tristam Shandy* and other pieces of literature with her.[22]

---

[19] TJ to Chastellux, 7 June, 1785.
[20] Cynthia A. Kierner, *Martha Jefferson Randolph, Daughter of Monticello: Her Life and Times* (Chapel Hill: The University of North Carolina Press, Kindle Edition 2017), 45–46.
[21] Cynthia Kierner, *Martha Jefferson Randolph, Daughter of Monticello,* 26.
[22] Cynthia Kierner, *Martha Jefferson Randolph, Daughter of Monticello,* 46.

He never seems to have believed, however, that women would or should be freed from the "circumstances of birth" in fulfilling their biological role because the very survival of men and women depended upon their fulfilling their role as mothers and wives. Most American men in the eighteenth century shared this view, though some, like Benjamin Rush, a signer of the Declaration of Independence, and Noah Webster, author of the American dictionary, each supported a more strenuous academic education for women than was generally offered in most schools that were open to young girls at that time. But as Kierner says in comparing Jefferson to Rush and Webster, "Though Jefferson shared their belief that education prepared girls to be better mothers and wives, he never discerned a political significance in women's domestic role, and consequently, unlike them, he never saw the education of females as a public responsibility or objective."[23]

In regard to the education of young men, Jefferson continued to view human nature as a "natural" rather than an "artificial" development. In his letter to John Adams (28 Oct. 1813), Jefferson agreed with Adams that there was a natural aristocracy among men based on individual virtue and talent. "The natural aristocracy I consider as the most precious gift of nature for the instruction, the trusts, and government of society."

Perhaps the most important understanding to be gained of Jefferson's view of human nature is contained in that 1813 letter to John Adams. It expresses the opinion that the nature of man had been assigned to him without regard to the human circumstances in which he might be placed due to the wealth or position of his parents, but their proper development and use were responsibilities of society as well as of the individual. It is this combined effort to free man from past conditions or circumstances of birth while charging society with the proper development of this natural aristocracy that makes Jefferson's view of human nature more complex than the views of most political thinkers who preceded him. He designed his educational system to sort out this natural aristocracy among men, so that "worth and genius would thus have been sought out from every condition of life, and completely prepared by education for defeating the competition of wealth and birth for public trusts."

Because of his belief in original endowments as a "gift of nature," he did not believe that all men could benefit equally from education. He writes to Cornelius Blatchly (21 Oct. 1822), "That every man shall be made virtuous, by any process whatever is, indeed, no more to be expected, than that every tree shall be made to bear fruit." He harbored no illusions about educating the masses other than at a very elementary level "three years gratis" so that all citizens of the republic could be self-sufficient and participate in voting and in the

---

[23] Cynthia Kierner, *Martha Jefferson Randolph, Daughter of Monticello*, 46.

affairs of local governance, but equally as important, he proposed this early education as a means of determining the natural aristocracy and dismissing "the residue." Jefferson writes in *Notes on the State of Virginia*:

> These schools to be under a visitor who is annually to choose the boy of best genius in the school, of those whose parents are too poor to give them further education, and to send him forward to one of the grammar schools.... Of the boys thus sent in one year, trial is to be made at the grammar schools one or two years, and the best genius of the whole selected, and continued six years, and the residue dismissed. By this means twenty of the best geniuses will be raked from the rubbish annually, and be instructed, at the public expense, so far as the grammar schools go.[24]

Given present day concern with fairness and compensation as required parts of equal opportunity, Jefferson's provision for only "the boy of best genius" being chosen from among the families too poor to provide further education would hardly seem adequate to defeat the competition of wealth and birth for public trusts. Curti noted this difficulty in his consideration of Jefferson's educational plans. "Perhaps the greatest qualification of the democracy of his scheme ... lay in the fact that it failed to take account of the ability of the wealthy to maintain their status by providing all their children with educational advantages, irrespective of their native ability."[25] But he also suggested that even though Jefferson's plans may have been somewhat comprised by today's views of equal educational opportunity, they were revolutionary in their day. In short, Jefferson was doing what he could to help the poor and convince the wealthy to support some form of public education.

Thus, it is necessary to view Jefferson's educational plans in the light of his belief in innate abilities and endowments as the essence of the nature of man and to view them in the perspective of what constituted a democratic concept in the eighteenth century. J.R. Pole wrote in *The Pursuit of Equality in American History* that "Jefferson had no illusions about equality of endowment, but he did believe that the state should use its powers in the public interest to equalize opportunity."[26]

Jefferson's educational policy was designed to reflect his belief in innate qualities and to allow each person to receive "an education proportioned to the condition and pursuits of

---

[24] Thomas Jefferson, *Notes on the State of Virginia*, in Saul K. Padover, The Complete Jefferson (New York: Duell, Sloan and Pearce, 1943), 667.

[25] Merle Curti, *Social Ideas of American Educators* (Patterson, New Jersey: Pageant Books, 1959), 42.

[26] J. R. Pole, *The Pursuit of Equality in American History* (Berkeley: University of California Press, 1978), 120.

his life."[27] The educational opportunity was not designed to determine what these pursuits might be; nature had made this determination. Jefferson's concern was to allow nature's distinctions to emerge. Thus, he stated in his Bill for the More General Diffusion of Knowledge the following rationale for public education:

> Whence it becomes expedient for promoting the publick happiness that those persons, whom nature hath endowed with genius and virtue, should be rendered by liberal education worthy to receive, and able to guard the sacred deposit of the rights and liberties of their fellow citizens, and that they should be called to that charge without regard to wealth, birth or other accidental condition or circumstance.[28]

Jefferson's belief in the assigned nature of man and in the necessity of a democratic society to "free" this nature for its proper use led him to propose the first truly public system of education based on his ideas of what constituted an equal educational opportunity. While holding to a belief in the assigned nature of man, he recognized that this assignment had been made democratically and that unless society provided the equal opportunities for its development, this talent might be wasted. Because the nature of man was based on innate endowments, rather than the circumstances of birth, equal educational opportunity was required to release human ability and talents. As Boyd explained in his explanation of Jefferson's Bill for the More General Diffusion of Knowledge, its revolutionary feature was "that in order to permit such a natural aristocracy to flourish freely, it would remove all economic, social, or other barriers that would interfere with nature's distribution of genius or virtue."[29] This was the revolutionary part of Jefferson's view of the nature of man and the foundation for his concept of an "Academical Village" based on the natural rights of man.

---

[27] TJ to Peter Carr, 7 Sept. 1814.
[28] Thomas Jefferson, Bill for the General Diffusion of Knowledge, This bill was included in the report of the committee on the revisal of the laws of Virginia, 1779. It is discussed in Julian P. Boyd, (ed.), *The Papers of Thomas Jefferson* (Princeton, New Jersey: Princeton University Press, 1950-, Vol. 2, 526-534.
[29] Boyd, (ed.), *The Papers of Thomas Jefferson,* vol. 2, 534.

# Mr. Jefferson's Law School

Richard E. Dixon

As early as 1778, Thomas Jefferson believed that the guardians of his Republic would be lawyers. His insight for mass education of the public found expression in Bill 79, "Bill for the More General Diffusion of Knowledge," prepared while he was a member of the Committee of Revisors of the laws of Virginia. He recites in the preamble:

> Whereas it is generally true that that people will be happiest whose laws are best, and are best administered, and that laws will be wisely formed, and honestly administered, in proportion as those who form and administer them are wise and honest; whence it becomes expedient for promoting the publick happiness that those person, whom nature hath endowed with genius and virtue should be rendered by liberal education worthy to receive, and able to guard the sacred deposit of the rights and liberties of their fellow citizens.[1]

The bill was first presented to the General Assembly in 1778, and again in 1786 while Jefferson was in Paris, but both times it failed of adoption. He wrote George Wythe on August 13, 1786, "I think by far the most important bill in our whole code is that for the diffusion of knowlege among the people. No other sure foundation can be devised for the preservation of freedom, and happiness." An education bill establishing public grammar schools was eventually passed in 1796, but it did not address Jefferson's concept of a tier of schools that would create an educated public.

---

[1] Thomas Jefferson, Bill for the More General Diffusion of Knowledge, *Thomas Jefferson, Writings*, ed. Merrill D. Peterson (New York, Library of America, 1984), 365.

## Rise of the Lawyer Class

There were no university law schools during the Colonial Era when Jefferson trained for the law (1760–1765). There were three paths that could be followed in order to be accepted by the courts as a lawyer.[2] One was to "read for the law," which would usually require a practicing lawyer as a mentor, for advice and access to law books. In the hindsight of his law career, he seemed to prefer this method (TJ to John Garland Jefferson, 11 June 1790), although he had followed the second method.

The second method, was to apprentice oneself to a practicing lawyer who would provide law books that could be studied and practical experience in the law office. Jefferson was an apprentice under George Wythe, one of Virginia's most notable attorneys.

The third was to study at the Inns of Court in England, which was an option closed to most because of the cost involved. It is a paradox that the Inns of Court lawyers, who did not have an exceptional legal education, looked down on the Virginia "country lawyers." The Inns of Court were not educational schools, but were mostly social and professional clubs. They conveyed a certain prestige because "graduates" were entitled to "argue in the high courts of justice in Westminster and to practice in any of the courts of the colony of Virginia."[3]

A proprietary law school in Litchfield, Connecticut was established about the close of the revolution and was in operation until 1833. Litchfield is sometimes mistakenly referred to as the forerunner to the Yale Law School.[4] There were perhaps four or five of these private "law schools" in Virginia, run by a single lawyer as a means of additional income.

It is doubtful whether Jefferson was aware of the curriculum or method of instruction in any of these schools when he became governor of Virginia in 1799 and was elected a member of the Board of Visitors of William & Mary College. His ideas on legal education had continued to develop during his years as a practicing lawyer. Neither lawyers nor judges were well thought of in the years leading up to the revolution, but lawyers in Virginia had emerged from the conflict as acknowledged leaders of the separation from Great Britain.[5] It was natural that Jefferson would look to them as the guardians of the nascent constitutional republic.

---

[2] James P. White, "Legal Education in the Era of Change," *Duke Law Journal*, Vol. 1987, No. 2, Legal Education (April 1987) 292; Richard E. Dixon, "A Lawyer's Path to a Legal Philosophy," *Thomas Jefferson and Philosophy: Essays on the Philosophical Cast of Jefferson's Writings*, ed. M. Andrew Holowchak, (Lanham: Lexington Books, 2014) 16-17.

[3] W. Hamilton Bryson, *The History of Legal Education in Virginia*, William & Mary Law School Scholarship Repository, 1979), 155.

[4] "The First Law School in America," *The Journal of Education*, Vol. 50, No. 13, 1247 (October 5, 1899), 231.

[5] A.G. Roeber, *Faithful Magistrates and Republican Lawyers* (Chapel Hill: University of North Carolina Press, 1981), 158.

Prior to Jefferson's selection to the Board of Visitors, there had been public agitation for the law to be taught at the College of William & Mary and for a major revamping of the curriculum.[6] He recounted in his *Autobiography* that he effected a change in the college by "abolishing the Grammar school, and the two professorships of Divinity & Oriental languages, and substituting a professorship of Law & Police, one of Anatomy Medicine, and Chemistry, and one of Modern languages."[7] Jefferson had great support in changing the curriculum and direction of the school from James Madison, president of the College and a cousin of the 4th president. The creation of the law professorship was not intended solely for the preparation of a legal career. William Blackstone, John Locke, and others had urged the study of law as a part of a gentleman's liberal education. Knowledge of the laws of society were necessary in order to manage estates, draft wills, and serve the public as jurors, justices of the peace and legislators.[8]

George Wythe, Jefferson's mentor and great friend, became the "professor of law and police," and the College of William & Mary is generally acknowledged as the first American law school.[9] Because of Jefferson's close association with Wythe, he is generally thought to have selected him. There is no doubt that Jefferson desired Wythe have the post, but Wythe was elected by the Board of Visitors, on which sat two other men who were signers of the Declaration of Independence with Wythe.

In addition to the legal studies, Wythe created a moot court system for the practice of litigation and a legislative body for an understanding of parliamentary procedure, consistent with Jefferson's vision that lawyers would be the future guardians of the nation. The sessions were held in the old Capitol building, after the capital was moved to Richmond. In order to receive the Bachelor of Law degree, a student was also to have the requisite for Bachelor of Arts and "must moreover be well acquainted with civil history, both ancient and modern, and particularly with municipal law and police."[10]

A number of factors, including the death of his wife, dissension in the faculty, and the efforts of the church to reassert its influence in the administrative affairs of the college, led Wythe to leave his long association with Williamsburg. In 1777, he accepted an appointment as a judge on the High Court of Chancery in Richmond. When the judiciary was reorganized

---

[6] W. Hamilton Bryson, *The History of Legal Education in Virginia*, 170–171.
[7] Thomas Jefferson, *Autobiography Writings*, 45.
[8] W. Hamilton Bryson, *The History of Legal Education in Virginia*, 167.
[9] The odd term "police" is derived from the Greek word "polis," which is normally used to indicate the ancient Greek city-states, like Classical Athens and its contemporaries, and thus is often translated as "city-state."
[10] Robert M. Hughes, "William and Mary: The First American Law School," *The William and Mary Quarterly*, Vol. 2, No. 1, Jan. 1922), 42. This article contains an interesting exchange of letters over the question whether the University of Pennsylvania was the first publicly established law school in the United States.

in 1788, he was appointed as the sole judge (Chancellor) of the Chancery Court of Virginia. He was succeeded as the professor of law at William & Mary by a former student St. George Tucker who annotated Blackstone's Commentaries for American consumption. It became such a "satisfactory textbook" that it "tended to encourage the apprenticeship method of instruction."[11]

Jefferson soon left to become minister plenipotentiary to France and after his return five years later his efforts became directed to national office. The reforms that he and Wythe had tried to institute gradually eroded. He did not believe this would be the place he could raise a class of educated lawyers to foster a self-reliant and free society. His concept of schools which reached out to all citizens on the lower levels and gradually made available higher education to the most capable appeared to be a dream unrealized.

In 1817, Harvard established what came to be known as the "university law school." Yale did the same in 1824. These law schools were part of the university system but basically followed the Litchfield model in which legal study and training was separate from a liberal arts education and other educational disciplines. The law school which Jefferson envisioned was based on a different pedagogical concept.

Thomas Jefferson's career as a lawyer, begun in 1767, was a relatively short eight years, but along with his apprenticeship under George Wythe, it informed his conception of how a lawyer should be trained. Jefferson believed that a study for the law was part of a broad-based liberal education. In various letters, Jefferson detailed the extensive study required and the necessity for a lawyer to be imbued with the culture of the society, a familiarity with the current science, a grasp of the constitutional basis for a social order, as well as a clear understanding of common and statutory law with attention to the sciences, history, and literature. He had long mapped out a plan of study with young aspirants for the law who sought his counsel.[12]

## Central College

As the seventy-one year old Jefferson rode through Charlottesville in March, 1814, quite by chance, the story goes, he was invited to a meeting of men who were interested in resuscitating an older plan for the creation of Albemarle Academy.[13] Jefferson agreed to

---

[11] John Ritchie, *The First Hundred Years: A Short History of the School of Law of the University Of Virginia for the Period 1826-1926* (Charlottesville: University Press of Virginia, 1978), 4.

[12] TJ to John Garland Jefferson, 11 June 1790 and TJ to John Minor, 30 Aug. 1814; See Richard E Dixon, "Colonial Lawyer," *The Journal of Thomas Jefferson's Life and Times*, Vol 1, No 1, 2017, 41.

draw the plans for a new building. During this process, he visualized the future path for a new university. A year later, he began his long association with Joseph Carrington Cabell, a senator from Albemarle County, who presented Jefferson's plan to the General Assembly for a college based on the education bill passed in 1796. On October 6, 1817, the cornerstone for Pavilion VII[14] of Central College was laid with Thomas Jefferson, James Madison, and James Monroe among those in attendance.

Just a day later, the first faculty member chosen was the professor of law. He was proposed by Jefferson, so the Visitors for Central College selected Thomas Cooper as a professor of chemistry and a professor of law. Cooper was a lawyer and a doctor who had held professorships at Dickinson College, University of Pennsylvania, and College of South Carolina. However, it was revealed that he was an adherent to Socianism. Joseph Cabell confided to his brother in a letter of March 21, 1820 that he feared Cooper "will do the University infinite injury." Although Cooper continued to have Jefferson's support, he was quietly set aside.[15]

In the winter of 1817-1818, Cabell submitted to the General Assembly Jefferson's Bill for Establishing a System of Public Education, which was essentially the same plan Jefferson had formulated in 1778. The bill failed, but the creation of a new state university was approved to be called "The University of Virginia." This led to the creation of the Rockfish Gap Commission and an internal struggle in the General Assembly among those who had their favorite schools or preferred locations where the university would be located.[16] After a contentious session, the General Assembly, on January 25, 1819, made Central College the site of the new University. The first Visitors of the University of Virginia were appointed: Thomas Jefferson, James Madison, Chapman Johnson, James Breckenridge, Robert B. Taylor, John H. Cocke, and Joseph C. Cabell. When Jefferson received the news that he had his new University of Virginia, he replied modestly, "I sincerely join in the general joy."[17] The Visitors elected Jefferson as the first Rector.

---

[13] Philip Alexander Bruce, *History of the University Of Virginia 1819-1919: The Lengthened Shadow of One Man*, Vol. 1 (New York, The Macmillan Company, 1920), 121.

[14] It became the modern Colonnade Club.

[15] Philip Alexander Bruce, *History of the University Of Virginia 1819-1919: The Lengthened Shadow of One Man*, Vol. 1, 200-5. Socianism denies the doctrines of the Trinity and the deity of Christ.

[16] Philip Alexander Bruce, *History of the University Of Virginia 1819-1919: The Lengthened Shadow of One Man*, Vol. 1, 206-9.

[17] Philip Alexander Bruce, *History of the University Of Virginia 1819-1919: The Lengthened Shadow of One Man*, Vol.1, 235.

## Building the Faculty

In October, 1824, the Board of Visitors adopted eight independent schools which would form the University. Each school would have its own building and the professors would be responsible to the Rector and the Board of Visitors. Students would enroll in the various schools, but would be free to take courses in the other schools. They were required to take at least three classes to take advantage of their time.[18] The term "schools" was one that Jefferson used. Although this was later changed 1862 to "department," the term "school" remained an unofficial description.[19]

Jefferson saw "the high qualifications of our professors as the only means by which we could give to our institution splendor and preeminence over all it's [sic] sister-seminaries. The only question therefore we can ever ask ourselves, as to any candidate, will be, Is he the most highly qualified?" (TJ to Cabell, 3 Feb. 1824).

Jefferson had previously written Cabell (28 Dec. 1822) that he also saw in his architecture the "distinguished scale of it's [sic] structure and preparation" a permanence that would draw to it the best students and the best professors. Otherwise, "foreign scholars of celebrity would hardly be willing to accept chairs in so new an institution."[20] Philip Alexander Bruce questions this assumption by Jefferson on the basis that the architecture or accommodations were not an issue in the negotiations with the professors that agreed to come to the University.

Jefferson understood that the creation of the University faced difficult odds. It would open with no immediate reputation, and most importantly there were no distinguished alumni to carry proof of its worth out into the world. It must immediately function successfully in all three areas of architecture, student body and teaching. There was still continued opposition in the General Assembly to locating the new university in Charlottesville. Jefferson observed to Cabell that a "proposal to move Wm & Mary College to Richmond, with all its present funds, and to add to it a medical school, is nothing more nor less than to move the University (TJ to Cabell, 22 Dec. 1824).

All efforts to find professors were futile. By the time the new university was chartered no professors had been retained.[21] Except for the professor of law and professor of ethics, it was decided to explore the possibilities for the faculty in Europe. This mission was given

---

[18] John S. Patton, Jefferson, Cabell and the University of Virginia, (Neale Publishing Company, 1906), 325.
[19] John Ritchie, xiv; The School of Law became the official term in 1952.
[20] Philip Alexander Bruce, History of the University Of Virginia 1819-1919: The Lengthened Shadow of One Man, Vol. 1, 243.
[21] John S. Patton, *Jefferson, Cabell and the University of Virginia,* 82.

to Francis Walker Gilmer, whose health was questionable at the time of his appointment. He was known by Jefferson since his early childhood and was a product of the same social class. He was a brilliant law apprentice in the office of William Wirt and later opened his own law office in Winchester. When Wirt moved to Washington to become attorney general, Gilmer moved to Richmond to accept his practice.[22]

There was much consternation over Gilmer's mission to Europe with the public wondering why professors could not be found in America. Even John Adams questioned Jefferson, in a letter of January 22, 1825: "I do believe there are sufficient scholars in America to fill your Professorships and Tutorships with more active ingenuity, and independent minds, than you can bring from Europe."

When the first session opened on March 7, 1825, the five "foreign" professors were in attendance, but the three Americans had not yet arrived. Cabell was inordinately pleased with the "corps of professors" and wrote to Jefferson that he felt the "University will advance with rapid strides and throw into the rear all the other seminaries" (25 May 1825).

## Finding a Law Professor

It was earlier agreed between Jefferson and Cabell that the chair of law must be filled by an American (Cabell to TJ, 16 Apr. 1824). The Visitors adopted a resolution at its meeting on March 4, 1825, "to pay special attention to the principles of government" which are not "incompatible with those on which the Constitution of the state, and of the United States, are genuinely based"[23]

One of the earliest suggestions for the law professorship by Cabell, with Cocke's concurrence, was Jefferson's nephew, Dabney Carr. He was then Chancellor, a prestigious judgeship, formerly held by George Wythe (Cabell to TJ, 29 Jan. 1824). Jefferson seemed to sense that his relationship with Carr was the motive behind Cabell's suggestion. He responded that Carr was "one of the best... the dearest of living men," that he had "ever looked on him as a son." These factors said Jefferson, "can never enter into the question of his qualifications as a Professor of the University" (TJ to Cabell, 3 Feb. 1824). It is not clear whether Carr was offered the position, but if so, he refused it. Later, when the Visitors were in a quandary over filling this position, Madison again raised his name with Jefferson but received "a silent reception" (Madison to Cocke, 13 Apr. 1825).

---

[22] Philip Alexander Bruce, *History of the University Of Virginia 1819–1919: The Lengthened Shadow of One Man*, Vol. 1, 342.
[23] John Ritchie, *The First One Hundred Years*, 8.

It was Jefferson's hope that the law professorship would go to Francis Walker Gilmer. Before he sailed, the Visitors gave him the option of Professor of Law or of Moral Philosophy. While in Edinburgh, Gilmer wrote that he could not accept $1500 but needed $2000 and in a letter to Chapman Johnson (August, 1824) suggested that "if you would make me president or something it would be a great inducement."[24] This proposal was apparently not considered by the Visitors, and after Gilmer returned, he wished to pursue a more public life. When his health continued to decline he decided the least onerous life of a professor might be better for him and lent an "attentive ear to Mister Jefferson's solicitation." His tentative acceptance was abrogated when his condition worsened. There is some dispute whether he reconsidered because of declining health, or because he felt he was recovering, but Jefferson still harbored hope, even up to Gilmer's death, of his recovery (TJ to Gilmer, 23 Jan. 1826). He died a month later on February 25, 1826.

The law professorship was next offered to Henry St. George Tucker, who at that time conducted a proprietary law school in Winchester. He was a "man of uncommon talents, a lawyer of extraordinary learning, and in disposition remarkable for his genial qualities, sense of humor, pure spirit, and perfect uprightness." He declined for a number of reasons, but apparently the main issue was the salary.[25]

The difficulty in finding a law professor who was satisfactory to the Visitors and to Jefferson is indicated by Madison's letter to Jefferson of January 25, 1826. Madison reviews the unsuccessful efforts to obtain a consent from Barbour, Dade, Rives, Preston, Robertson, or Terrell. One month later, Madison shows his frustration with the inability to fill the law professorship writing Jefferson that "the awkward state of the law professorship is truly distressing, but seems to be without immediate remedy" (24 Feb. 1826).

William H. Cabell suggested in March, 1826 the name of William Wirt, then Attorney General of the United States. He said that offering him the presidency of the University, as a means of increasing his salary, would be an enticement.[26] Patton concludes that there was "some expectation" that Wirt would accept the chair.[27] Jefferson was in strong opposition. He believed that the faculty should select a chairman from their number, who would not have administrative authority over the other schools. Perhaps in frustration that the law school had not opened with the other schools, Jefferson finally consented. He

---

[24] Philip Alexander Bruce, *History of the University of Virginia, 1819-1919: The Lengthened Shadow of One Man*, Volume 2 (The Macmillan Company 1920), 26.

[25] Philip Alexander Bruce, *History of the University Of Virginia 1819-1919: The Lengthened Shadow of One Man*, Vol. 1, 27.

[26] Philip Alexander Bruce, *History of the University Of Virginia 1819-1919: The Lengthened Shadow of One Man*, Vol. 2, 29.

[27] John S. Patton, *Jefferson, Cabell and the University of Virginia*, 110.

did provide in the minute book precise details of the new president's function and responsibilities and also enumerated his "protests against both the expediency and validity of the establishment of this office."[28] Bruce suggests that Jefferson consented because he "considered it to be his personal and official duty to suppress the feeling of opposition which he had entertained."[29]

Although Wirt did decline the position, he recommended that the Visitors appoint John Taylor Lomax. He had a well regarded reputation from his practice of law in Fredericksburg, and John S. Patton credits him with a "profound knowledge of the law"[30] Jefferson notified Lomax by letter of April 12, 1826 that, it is "with great pleasure that I inform you by an unanimous vote of the rector & visitors of the University of Virginia they have appointed you professor of the school of law." Lomax became the first Dean of the law school, which he considered "one of the highest stations on earth."[31]

On this turn of events, Cabell wrote to Jefferson (6 Apr. 1826) that, "Wirt would not accept the law chair. Mr. Lomax therefore is the Professor, & the system will remain as you desired." Lomax was a consistent proponent of the legal thought of Jefferson and Madison that upheld the sovereignty of the states against the federal courts. He taught by the lecture method and followed the textbooks prescribed by the Board of Visitors.[32] Lomax withdrew in 1830 to accept the judgeship of the Fredericksburg Circuit Court, but even then continued to operate a private law school. The University would operate for a hundred years without a president, just as Jefferson envisioned.

## Restrictions on the Law Professor

Jefferson acknowledged that in the selection of textbooks the Visitors were not as well-versed in the various subjects and science as the professors and they would be permitted to choose their own textbooks. However, in the case of the law school Jefferson demurred: "There is one branch in which we are the best judges, in which heresies may be taught, of

---

[28] John S. Patton, *Jefferson, Cabell and the University of Virginia*, 110–13.
[29] Philip Alexander Bruce, *History of the University Of Virginia 1819-1919: The Lengthened Shadow of One Man*, Vol. 2, 31.
[30] John S. Patton, *Jefferson, Cabell and the University of Virginia*, 114.
[31] Philip Alexander Bruce, *History of the University Of Virginia 1819-1919: The Lengthened Shadow of One Man*, Vol. 2, 32.
[32] Philip Alexander Bruce, *History of the University Of Virginia 1819-1919: The Lengthened Shadow of One Man*, Vol. 2, 103.

so interesting a character to our own state and to the (United States) as to make it a duty in us to lay down the principles which shall be taught' (TJ to Cabell, 3 Feb. 1825).

Jefferson "felt that he was as much of a specialist as a man who might be chosen to teach those subjects, but he was fully determined that such principles alone should be imparted in both as were satisfactory to his convictions."[33] General Cocke had earlier "emphasized the intention of the Board of Visitors to confine the selection of incumbents for the chairs of ethics and law to American citizens."[34] They followed Jefferson's lead that a foreign professor would not sufficiently understand the social and political principles which were uniquely American.

When Gilmer withdrew his intention to accept the position of law professor, Jefferson communicated his concern to him about choosing a "Gothic lawyer," one who did not have an academic background, and who accepted the principle of "consolidation" (20 Jan 1825). This became a rigid test for Jefferson on who might now be selected. His admonition to Cabell, which he also communicated to James Madison, was very explicit that he was opposed to "a Richmond lawyer," or a believer in "quondam federalism, now Consolidation." His solution to guard against the "diffusion of that poison" was by prescribing the texts that could be used (TJ to Cabell, 3 Feb. 1825).

Jefferson had proposed the writings of Algernon Sidney and John Locke, the Declaration of Independence, the Federalist, and the Virginia Resolution of 1799. Madison agreed that "the true doctrines of liberty," should be "inculcated" into the students of the law. Although he agreed with most of the selections by Jefferson for textbooks, he urged caution with respect to the "Virginia Document of 1799" in conveying a partisan attitude which might "excite prejudice against the University." He also suggested adding the Inaugural Address and the Farewell Address of George Washington (8 Feb. 1825).

In spite of his stance to control the curriculum, no one of his generation did more in the early republic to foster freedom of the mind and expression than Jefferson.[35]

---

[33] Philip Alexander Bruce, *History of the University Of Virginia 1819–1919: The Lengthened Shadow of One Man*, Vol. 1, 328.
[34] Philip Alexander Bruce, *History of the University Of Virginia 1819–1919: The Lengthened Shadow of One Man*, Vol. 2, 19.
[35] Dumas Malone, *Jefferson and His Time: Sage of Monticello* (Boston: Little Brown and Co., 1981), 418.

## Early Curriculum Plans

Many law students had limited income and looked on their education as preparation for a trade. They were anxious to complete their studies. The first session consisted of "all the important branches of municipal law" and the second session was a deeper analysis of their application. John Taylor Lomax was sympathetic to their efforts to complete their law training as quickly as possible. The studies gradually shifted under Lomax who selected what he felt were the "most approved and suitable English textbooks," i.e., (1) Blackstone's *Commentaries*, (2) Cruise's *Law of Real Property*, (3) Selwyn's *Abstract of the Law of Nisi Prius*, and (4) Muddock's *Chancery*. Lomax also recommended to the Visitors an "academic course of law" which was a survey of American jurisprudence.[36]

The law students were generally older and objected to required examinations which published the names of the successful in the paper. They also resisted the uniforms required by the school, which required the additional expenditure of funds for clothing which they would only wear for a short time. It was also onerous to them that a proctor would manage their money. Lomax was able to convince the Visitors to relieve these requirements and to allow the law students to live off-campus.[37]

The uniform code required the uniform to be worn on the Sabbath, during examinations, public exhibitions, or whenever the student left the campus. The coat was high at the neck with a braided standing collar, single breasted waistcoat and pantaloons with a single stripe. Apparently, the uniform law was instituted to enforce "economical habits among the students, the prevention of invidious distinctions, and the discouragement of frivolous taste." It was to refute the idea that the University was only for the wealthy and to retain the goodwill of the General Assembly on which the University was dependent.[38]

## Degrees Awarded

Jefferson thought of the university's program as a graduate program and no honorary degrees would be bestowed. Degrees were restricted to the doctrinal, academic, or

---

[36] Philip Alexander Bruce, *History of the University Of Virginia 1819-1919: The Lengthened Shadow of One Man*, Vol. 2, 102-3.
[37] Philip Alexander Bruce, *History of the University Of Virginia 1819-1919: The Lengthened Shadow of One Man*, Vol. 2, 104.
[38] Philip Alexander Bruce, *History of the University Of Virginia 1819-1919: The Lengthened Shadow of One Man*, Vol. 2, 247.

vocational. In the beginning the vocational comprises the doctoral and master's degrees which gradually encompassed other professional degrees such as bachelor of laws. Jefferson opposed honorary degrees since "every degree bestowed by the institution should be a proof of merit" awarded for classroom performance. Jefferson's resistance was likely based on his aversion to artificial titles or aristocratic attitudes. However, after Jefferson's death, the Visitors established the traditional degrees of bachelor's, master's and doctoral.[39]

In 1829, the faculty recommended a number of degrees including academic and professional degrees in the school of law. The academic degree would recite "graduate of the school of law." However, this did not entitle the recipient to become a member of the bar. The professional degree did entitle the holder to the title "Barrister of Law." The degree Bachelor of Law does not appear until July, 1840.[40]

## Conduct Unbecoming

Jefferson would not live to see his law school open, and in the year the University of Virginia did operate before his death one of his great regrets was the conduct in manners exhibited by the University students. Jefferson had believed that rules prescribing student conduct would be unnecessary, that students were thought to be already trained to exercise decorum and restraint. It soon became apparent that his confidence was misplaced. Drinking, gambling, serious pranks and assaults frequently occurred. This was in the age of the orderly duel and that caused many students to carry dirks and pistols which resulted in assaults and insults to professors.

Riotous conduct on October 1, 1825 required civilian authorities to restore order and led to multiple expulsions. At the meeting of the Visitors to consider this issue, two professors resigned. Jefferson tried to speak to the issue but was too overcome with emotion to continue. The solution was to establish a civil court called the Court of the University with the Dean of the Law School as the judge of the court. This court was not created until October, 1826, after Jefferson's death.[41]

---

[39] Philip Alexander Bruce, *History of the University Of Virginia 1819-1919: The Lengthened Shadow of One Man*, Vol. 2, 136.
[40] Philip Alexander Bruce, *History of the University Of Virginia 1819-1919: The Lengthened Shadow of One Man*, Vol. 2, 139.
[41] John S. Patton, *Jefferson, Cabell and the University of Virginia*, 133.

In spite of the efforts of the faculty to create diversions for the students, who were removed from centers of population, their riotous conduct continued for at least another 30 years. At one point it resulted in the death in 1840 of Professor of Law, John A.G. Davis, who was trying to maintain order during a disturbance and was shot and killed by a student. During this period, there were expulsions and students were charged with misdemeanors, but it is not fully explained by historians of this era why this type of conduct could not be curtailed.

## Father of the American Law School

One of the tributes to Jefferson on the founding of the University was a comment from Wilson Cary Nicholas, that "your college is made the University of Virginia. I call it your, as you are its real founder, its commencement can only be ascribed to you. [sic] to your exertions & influence its being adopted can only the [sic] attributed" (25 Jan 1819).

When the Marquis de Lafayette came to the United States for his famous visit in 1825, he had dinner with Jefferson at the Rotunda before the school was opened. One of the toasts honored Jefferson as the "founder the University of Virginia." John Ritchie, in his study of the University law school, also proclaimed that "not only was he the father of the University but he was also the father of the modern, American law school."[42]

The School of Law at the University of Virginia has operated continuously to the present day and it has become one of the great law schools in the United States.[43]

---

[42] John Ritchie, *The First One Hundred Years*, 1.
[43] For a timeline to the modern era, see *A History of the School of Law at the University Of Virginia*, https://www.scribd.com/document/65808162/History-of-UVA-Law-to-1959m, accessed 21 Sept. 20

# Thomas Jefferson, Medicine, and the University of Virginia

## White McKenzie Wallenborn

THOMAS JEFFERSON, TRULY A MAN for all seasons, was deeply involved in medicine. How he found time for this interest is truly amazing when we consider that he spent over 35 years in the service to our young country, and put much effort into his many other fields of expertise, which included architecture, scientific farming, botany, archeology, paleontology, and astronomy, to name but a few.

As a young man, he developed strong opinions about health and exercise. During his long and productive life, Thomas Jefferson promoted some earl advances in preventive medicine, worked toward better public health in Virginia and in the nation, and—with his creation of the Medical School at the University of Virginia—had a profound effect on how medicine was taught across the United States.

Jefferson's influence was evident despite his suffering from some unique maladies, and despite his holding strong, negative opinions about doctors and how medicine was practiced at the time. "The state of medicine is worse than that of total ignorance," he wrote to William Green Mumford (18 June 1799): "Whenever I saw three physicians together," Jefferson told Dr. Robley Dunglison, "I looked up to discover whether there was a turkey buzzard in the neighborhood."[1] To Caspar Wistar, M.D., he wrote (21 June 1807): "Presumptuous bands of medical tyros, let loose upon the world, destroy more human life in one year than all the Robin Hoods, Cartouches, and MacHeaths do in a century."

Although he mistrusted most physicians, he did have faith in a few: Dr. George Gilmer of Pen Park, father of Francis Walker Gilmer whom Jefferson sent to England to recruit faculty for the University of Virginia; Dr. Thomas Walker, who had been Peter Jefferson's physician and is recognized for his original description of a new treatment for osteomyelitis;[2] Dr. Benjamin Rush of Philadelphia; and Dr. Robley Dunglison, first Professor of Medicine at the University of Virginia. However, his lack of confidence in other physicians was not

---

[1] Recollection by Dr. Robley Dunglison in his Personal Memoranda. See John M. Dorsey, *The Jefferson-Dunglison Letters* (Charlottesville: University of Virginia Press, 1960), 105.

complete because, when he consulted them, he would carefully follow their advice and take their prescribed medication.

Without doubt, Thomas Jefferson was a man of the Enlightenment. "To the men of the Enlightenment," wrote Bernard Bailyn, "their age was like the dawn of a new day in humanism, rationality, scientific methodology, and religious toleration, after a long night of superstition, intolerance, and misery."[3] Mr. Jefferson believed that there was a rational explanation for all phenomena and clearly felt that medicine was still in that "long night of superstition, intolerance, and misery."

Very early in his political career he began to take steps to correct this serious situation. After he was elected Governor of Virginia, he effected a change in the faculty at the College of William and Mary (c. 1779-1780) that initiated the first school of medicine in Virginia. This predated the establishment of Harvard Medical School by about three years. Unfortunately, Dr. James McClurg—the first Professor of Anatomy, Medicine, and Chemistry—resigned after four years and the medical school at William and Mary expired.[4]

As a young adult, Mr. Jefferson had developed an interest in the exciting possibilities of preventive medicine. While a college student at William and Mary he traveled, with some difficulty, from Williamsburg to Philadelphia to be vaccinated (or inoculated) against smallpox by Dr. William Shippen. This vaccination most likely comprised the live virus made from the pustules of smallpox infected patients.[5] (Edward Jenner's cowpox vaccine was not readily available until after 1798.)

Smallpox was a deadly disease in those days, able to wipe out entire slave populations, eradicate Indian tribes, and debilitate large armies. During the Revolutionary War, for example, British General Charles Cornwallis captured Jefferson's Elk Hill farm on the James River and took the slaves to Yorktown where almost all of them died from smallpox.

Jefferson, during this period, began working to improve public health. As governor of Virginia Jefferson voiced concerns with the improvement of sanitation, ventilation, water supplies, and disease prevention. Some years later he collaborated with Dr. Benjamin Waterhouse to develop a program of national vaccination.[6] Twenty years after the Revolution, Mr. Jefferson ordered Jenner's smallpox vaccine, and personally vaccinated his family and slaves at Monticello.[7]

---

[2] James O. Breeden, "The Medical World of Thomas Walker," *The Magazine of Albemarle County History*, Vol. 52, 1994, 24.
[3] Bernard Bailyn, "Ideological Origins," Personal Notes from Bailyn on Enlightenment.
[4] Dumas Malone, *Jefferson the Virginian* (Boston: Little, Brown and Company, 1948), 284-85.
[5] Dumas Malone, *Jefferson the Virginian* (Boston: Little, Brown and Company, 1848), 99.
[6] W.B. Blanton, *Medicine in Virginia in the Eighteenth Century* (Richmond: Garrett and Massie, 1931), 252.
[7] Jack McGlaughlin, *Jefferson and Monticello* (New York: Henry Holt and Co., Inc., 1988), 142.

## Thomas Jefferson, Abroad

Jefferson further pursued his interests in medicine, public health, and architecture while serving as Minister to France from 1784 to 1789. At that time in France, significant hospital design changes and preventive medicine programs were underway. Thomas Jefferson actively participated with many of his French peers in these efforts.

The d'Hotel-Dieu in Paris, a deathtrap of a hospital with a 20-30 percent mortality rate, is a perfect case in point. Its situation was simply appalling. The hospital was in an unhealthy location, held a crowded mass of 3,000 patients—four to six patients to a bed—and mixed diseases in the same wards and beds. Additionally, it was an unsafe environment—a potential fire hazard—providing insufficient and contaminated water to its unlucky inmates. The Paris Academy of Sciences recognized it as a source of contagion with its vitiated air, and pollution of the city water supply, and took the lead in bringing about much needed hospital reform.[8]

Thomas Jefferson was a very close friend of two of the men associated with the planning for these changes by the Paris Academy of Sciences, the Marquis de Cordocet and Pierre Samuel DuPont de Nemours (a Physiocrat and physician).[9]

Hospitals, thereafter, were to become "healing machines" for patient-citizens by the changing of their location, design, and operation. The new hospitals were to be of pavilion, or isolated-ward, design where patients could be segregated by disease and placed in separate beds. They were to be places where innovations in physics, chemistry, pathological anatomy, surgery, medical technology, sanitation, architecture, and hospital administration would be practiced.

Louis XVI ordered the construction of four such new hospitals. Each held 1,200 patient beds organized in twelve symmetrically parallel pavilions aligned along a main axis—six on either side of an open garden, with a central chapel building at its head—connected by covered walkways for convalescent patients. This design provided for improved ventilation, economy of space, efficiency, cleanliness, and safety, and, at the same time, reduced the risk of fire and contagion.

Inspection of Jefferson's layout for the University of Virginia shows plainly how it resembles the new hospitals in France. In a letter to Governor Wilson Cary Nicholas (2 Apr.

---

[8] Louis S. Greenbaum, "Thomas Jefferson, the Paris Hospitals, and the University of Virginia," *Eighteenth-Century Studies*, Vol. 26, No. 4, 1993.

[9] This same DuPont de Nemours had been vital in facilitating the 1783 Treaty of Paris that ended the Revolutionary War and was also involved in the negotiations leading to the Louisiana Purchase in 1803.

1816) of Virginia, Mr. Jefferson states that for his own academical village, he selected the village form rather than one large building "for reasons of fire, health, economy, peace, and quiet."

The new "healing machines" were an improvement in public health, but DuPont's ideas carried the matter one step further. He felt that dehospitalization of disease and poverty, by medical assistance at home, was healthier, cheaper, and more humane than hospital care.[10] Thomas Jefferson concurred. In his *Notes on the State of Virginia*, first published in May of 1785, Jefferson described the parish relief system of his state as the most effective, inexpensive, and compassionate scheme of self-help and home care. "Parish assistance and household relief by friends and neighbors is, without comparison, better than in a hospital," he wrote, "where the sick, the dying, and the dead are crammed together in the same rooms, and often in the same beds. Nature and kind nursing save a much greater proportion in our own plain way at a smaller expense, and with less abuse."[11]

## Jefferson and the Teaching of Medicine

Formal medical school education in the American colonies had its beginnings in 1765 with the formation of a medical department at the College of Pennsylvania. By 1820 there were thirteen medical schools in the United States.[12] Medical school in those days, consisted of two years, with two four month terms, followed by several years of preceptorship.

Todd Savitt, writing for the Virginia Medical Monthly in 1995, quoted Thomas Jefferson's June 21, 1807, letter to Dr. Caspar Wistar saying that he believed medical school instructors based their teachings too much upon speculative theories and too little on the realities of medical practice. Mr. Jefferson designed the medical curriculum at the University of Virginia to avoid these problems, and to fit the needs of a mostly rural American population. He insisted that medical theory be taught as an historical subject only, and ordered instruction to concentrate, rather, on the practical, fundamental problems of medicine. Under his system, no one would graduate from the University of Virginia as a physician.[13]

---

[10] Louis S. Greenbaum, "Thomas Jefferson, the Paris Hospitals, and the University of Virginia," 613.

[11] Thomas Jefferson, *Notes on the State of Virginia,* ed. William Peden (Chapel Hill: University of North Carolina Press, 1955), 133-34.

[12] Todd L. Savitt, "Jefferson's Vision of Medical Education and His Quest for a Professor of Medicine," *Virginia Medical Quarterly,* Vol. 122, No. 4, 1995, 246-47.

[13] Todd L. Savitt, "Jefferson's Vision of Medical Education and His Quest for a Professor of Medicine," 246.

This was to change, however, as the first four degrees conferred by the University, in 1828, were Doctor of Medicine degrees. (Incidentally, in 1831 one of Jefferson's grandsons, Benjamin Franklin Randolph, graduated from the University of Virginia as a Doctor of Medicine. One of the founders of the Martha Jefferson Hospital, in Charlottesville, Dr. William Mann Randolph, was a great-great-great-grandson of Thomas Jefferson.)

What Mr. Jefferson had proposed for the education of medical students was that, after they had qualified themselves within the other branches of science at the University of Virginia, they would then complete their course of preparation by attending clinical lectures for six or twelve months in Norfolk, where the United States already had an established hospital with an ample number of patients.[14]

Savitt further noted in his article that Mr. Jefferson argued for the abandonment of hypotheses in favor of sober facts, with the highest value set on clinical observation and the lowest on visionary theory. Thomas Jefferson felt that anatomy and clinical observation were the two major areas of medical education. "The only sure foundations of medicine," he wrote, "are an intimate knowledge of the human body and observations on the effects of medicinal substances on that body."[15]

Courses taught in the medical department at the University— according to the contract between the University and the first Professor of Medicine, Dr. Robley Dunglison— included anatomy, surgery, physiology, materia medica, pharmacy, and the history of the progress and theories of medicine from Hippocrates to the present. The new professor of medicine was allowed neither to have his own private practice, nor to teach clinical medicine, at least not with live patients. Francis Walker Gilmer, who was sent to England to recruit the faculty, encountered difficulty in procuring a professor of medicine when the applicants discovered that they would not be allowed to practice at, or outside, the University. This restriction was later changed by the Board of Visitors so that Robley Dunglison could treat Thomas Jefferson. Dunglison was "permitted to act as a consulting physician elsewhere, so timing these avocations, however, as to not interrupt the regular business of the school."[16]

When the University of Virginia enrolled its first students in March of 1825, twenty signed up for medical subjects. The Anatomical Theater, which Jefferson designed, was not yet completed so the first lectures in medicine were held at Robley Dunglison's residence, Pavilion X. (Incidentally, the Anatomical Theater is the only Jefferson-designed building that the University of Virginia has demolished—a tragedy.)

---

[14] Todd L. Savitt, "Jefferson's Vision of Medical Education and His Quest for a Professor of Medicine," 249.
[15] Todd L. Savitt, "Jefferson's Vision of Medical Education and His Quest for a Professor of Medicine," 246.
[16] John M. Dorsey, *The Jefferson-Duglinson Letters*, 44.

In April, 1826, the Board of Visitors passed a resolution stating that: "There be established in the University a Dispensary which shall be attached to the Medical school and shall be under the sole direction and government of the Professor of Medicine who shall attend personally at the anatomical theater, or such other place as he shall notify, from half-after-one to two o'clock on every Tuesday, Thursday, and Saturday, for the purpose of dispensing medical advice, vaccination, and aid in Surgical cases of ordinary occurrence, to applicants needing them. All poor, free persons disordered in body, topically or generally, applying for advice, shall receive it gratis; all others bond or free, shall receive it on payment of a half a dollar at each attendance, for use of the institution, and all persons shall be vaccinated gratis, and the students particularly shall be encouraged to be so, as a protection to the institution against the malady of the smallpox."[17]

The idea of a dispensary was apparently a joint decision by Thomas Jefferson and Robley Dunglison. As it developed, the University of Virginia established the first full-time state-supported university medical school clinical faculty in the United States. The comprehensive medical and scientific curriculum planned by Thomas Jefferson—with its emphasis on preclinical training and clinical instruction under the close supervision of medical school faculty—was accepted as the standard for instruction in American medical schools.

## "Here's to Your Health, Mr. Jefferson!"

"You may promise yourself everything but health," wrote Jefferson to grandson Thomas Mann Randolph, Jr. (6 July 1787), "without which there is no happiness." On July 21, 1787, he wrote to Thomas Mann Randolph: "The most uninformed mind, with a healthy body, is happier than the wisest valedictorian." For the most part, Thomas Jefferson was very healthy. Certainly his good health and longevity were related to his personal health regimen.

He was a strong advocate of exercise. As a college student at William and Mary, for example, he would jog precisely two miles every day. As an adult, Jefferson devoted to exercise the hours from one to three p.m. each day. He exercised regularly up to the last few weeks of his life. "Exercise and application," he wrote to his daughter, Martha Jefferson Randolph (28 Mar. 1781), "produce order in our affairs, health of body, cheerfulness of mind, and these make us precious to our friends."

---

[17] John M. Dorsey, *The Jefferson-Duglinson Letters*, 47.

"Exercise is to the body as reading is to the mind" was a frequent Jeffersonian statement. His commentary on his diet—that he consumed "little animal food, not as an aliment so much as a condiment for the vegetables, which constitute my principle diets"[18]—indicates that he was a person ahead of his time in healthy eating habits. As to the treatment of illnesses, Mr. Jefferson felt that nature, if left alone, would restore the natural balance which had been undone by disease. Doctors, he felt, interfered with this restorative process.

Mr. Jefferson partook of neither tobacco nor hard liquors. He discouraged visitors to Monticello from giving toasts after dinner because it encouraged them to drink more than they should. An operator of a Charlottesville boarding house once asked him to recommend beverages for college students and Mr. Jefferson replied that "their drink at all times [should] be water" because young stomachs needed "no stimulating drinks" and he believed "the habit of using them dangerous."[19] Wine, however, was his favorite beverage and his wine cellar probably contained the finest selection of European wines in this country.

Naturally, despite his many healthy habits, Thomas Jefferson did have a few bouts with illness. As a young man, for example he suffered frequently from colds, sinusitis, and bronchitis. Possibly upon the advice of George Wythe—and possibly from reading a book entitled Baynard on Cold Bathing—he began, at about the age of twenty-two, to place his feet in a bucket of cold water upon rising.[20] "I have for fifty years bathed my feet in cold water every morning," he wrote to James Maury (15 June 1815), "and have been remarkably exempted from colds (having had only one in every seven years of my life, on average)."

Jefferson also had severe, debilitating migraine-like headaches from early adulthood until sometime after he retired from politics. When he was serving as minister to France, for example, he was several times hampered by unrelenting headaches that completely disabled him for four to six weeks at a time. Fortunately, he found some relief at home. He painted the walls black in the South Square bed chamber, at Monticello, and would retire to this room when he was afflicted with migraines.

During his lifetime, Mr. Jefferson injured both of his wrists. He hurt his right wrist in Paris in 1786 when—while trying to impress Maria Cosway—he leaped across a wall, fell and fractured or dislocated it. Many years later, he fell off the North Terrace at Monticello and fractured his left wrist.

In his old age Thomas Jefferson was afflicted with several maladies. Rheumatism, for example, began causing him considerable discomfort in his seventies and this continued

---

[18] TJ to Dr. Vine Utley, 21 Mar. 1819.
[19] TJ to Dr. Vine Utley, 21 Mar. 1819.
[20] John M. Dorsey, *The Jefferson-Dunglinson Letters*, 99.

until his death. While trying to seek relief from this condition—by using the baths at Warm Springs in 1818—Jefferson developed several boil, or abscess, lesions of his buttocks which caused him great suffering. He had to endure four very painful days traveling home in a carriage. At first he was treated with topical sulfur and mercurials, and later, a mercurial compound by mouth which made him deathly ill. Only when he stopped the treatment did he recover.[21]

In 1819 Jefferson developed a painful swelling in his legs. His slaves, Isaac Jefferson and John Hemings, after bathing him and wrapping his legs, had to carry him in a hand barrow. Fortunately, the swelling did not hurt when Jefferson could get up and walk but it took, nonetheless, two months for him to recover.[21]

In October of 1824, about a week before the Marquis de Lafayette was to arrive for an eleven-day visit, Jefferson developed an imposthume, or abscess, of the jaw which was slow to heal and bothered his speech. As he got older, Jefferson complained of having difficulty hearing when in group conversation. His hearing was adequate, however, when speaking one-on-one. Was this presbycusis, a form of high frequency hearing loss in the elderly, or was it a late complication of having taken quinine, an ototoxic drug, in the form of Peruvian Bark (known as cinchona)? Probably it was a combination of the two. In his latter years, also, Jefferson was forced to rely on glasses, although he claimed he needed them only at night, or for small print. Apparently he had all of his teeth at the time of his death.

## Jefferson's Passing

Thomas Jefferson died, at age eighty-three, on July 4, 1826, at about 12:50 p.m. This was fifty years—almost to the hour—from the time he had handed the Declaration of American Independence to John Hancock for his signature. What was the cause of his death? It was probably a combination of several disorders. He was rather old and debilitated from rheumatism, and, for several years, he had at times suffered from severe, and unrelenting diarrhea. Also, for at least a year, Thomas Jefferson had had progressive trouble with urinary obstruction most likely from benign prostatic hypertrophy. (Some sources have postulated that Jefferson's ailment was prostatic cancer, but this is debatable.) Dr. Robley Dunglison had to make frequent trips up to Monticello to dilate Jefferson's urethra with a gum-type bougie, and more than likely this caused a significant urinary tract infection.

---

[21] Charles Campbell, *Memoirs of a Monticello Slave* (Charlottesville: University of Virginia Press, 1951), 44–45. This malady was, perhaps, glomerulonephritis, typhoid fever with phlebitis, tubular damage from his mercurial therapy, congestive heart failure, or parasitic lyphangitis.

(Thus, the combination of several factors: severe diarrhea, with resulting fluid and electrolyte imbalance and dehydration; a urethral obstruction, along with a significant urinary tract infection; and, finally, being bedridden for about ten days—during the last three days of which Mr. Jefferson was, for the most part, in a coma—probably caused a terminal postural-positional pneumonia.)

Jefferson's systems failed his once-strong body and he died in bed at Monticello, fittingly, on July the fourth. He had served his nation, and fellow men, well. After his death, the family found his instructions for his tombstone, and its epitaph. "On the faces of the obelisk," he had written, place "the following inscription and not a word more: Here was buried Thomas Jefferson, Author of the Declaration of Independence, Of the Statute of Virginia for Religious Freedom, and Father of the University of Virginia."

"Because of these," concluded his note, "as testimonials that I have lived, I wish most to be remembered." To that we might even add the following: Because of the beliefs and actions noted above, Thomas Jefferson was one of the principals in curing the ills of American medicine.

# Self and Selflessness

# Elite-Level Education and the Paradox of Public Service in a Jeffersonian Republic

M. Andrew Holowchak

THOMAS JEFFERSON STATES UNEQUIVOCALLY in numerous writings that in any form of "aristocratic" government—the worst of which is a hereditary kingship (TJ to John Adams, 28 Sept. 1787)—those empowered to serve as political leaders, even those well-intentioned, tend in time to forget the interests of the general citizenry. Instead, they indulge themselves in abuses of power, such as, he tells William Duane (28 Mar. 1811), "violating our dearest rights, the trial by jury, the freedom of the press, the freedom of opinion, civil or religious, or opening on our peace of mind or personal safety the sluices of terrorism, ... [or] raising standing armies."[1]

A Jeffersonian republic must have a certain structure to prevent a slide into tyranny or chaos. The structure Jefferson envisages is politically loose, yet naturally tight, as it is firmly rooted in human nature. Each person is born with a moral sense which perceives right action relatively unerringly, even in complex scenarios, and that sense of right action is the foundation of Jefferson's republican thinking.[2] Thus, the structure of a Jeffersonian republic aims at securing vital human rights—such as life, liberty, and pursuit of happiness—and the best security of those rights is election, directly by the morality-abiding citizenry, of the intellectual and moral elite to the offices of government.

In short, when a Jeffersonian republic functions rightly, the life and liberty of each citizen is protected, and the people are free to do as they please to do—chart their own path to happiness. When breathing the intemerate air of freedom, the general citizenry, following their untrammeled moral sense, will be as politically active as their time and talents allow, and the intellectual and moral elite will devote their life to public service through political offices, even at the expense of their personal affairs, or the practice of science.

And so, there is a built-in paradox to Jeffersonian republicanism. When and only when the people have liberty sufficient to do whatever they want to do, then the people will do what they ought to do. Concerning the intellectual and moral elite, when their liberty

---

[1] See also, e.g., TJ to James Madison, 18 Mar. 1785; TJ to John Adams, 28 Feb. 1796; and TJ to James Monroe, 11 June 1823.
[2] See M. Andrew Holowchak, *Thomas Jefferson, Moralist* (Jefferson, NC: McFarland, 2017), chap. 1.

is maximal and when they can cultivate the greatest sense of self, they will, through a heightened sense of duty, act selflessly—viz., for the good of the whole. Why? The answer lies in Jefferson's views on educating the elite.

## "The greatest good..."

In Book IV of Republic (419a–420d), Plato structures his ideal polis on the division between laborers and guardians (functioning like police and a military force), and from the latter, over time, there arises a group of rulers or complete guardians, whose task it is to rule the polis. Plato through the mouth of Socrates delineates the lengthy process of education that guardians must undertake and describes their relatively austere, other-serving lifestyle.[3]

Having listened to the account of a guardians' austere lifestyle, Adeimantus challenges Socrates. "What would you say, Socrates, if someone told you that you are not making the guardians very happy and it is their own fault? They own the polis, but derive no good from that." The laborers own land, construct large and fine homes, possess gold and silver, entertain guests, make private sacrifices to the gods, and have numerous things in their houses. "Your guardians as merely inhabitants of the polis like mercenaries. All they do is watch over it."

The scenario is worse for those guardians who separate themselves from others and become rulers. They are educated in mathematics and dialectic till the age of 50 (the life-expectancy of a Greek then was 28[4]), when then they are in position to govern their polis. Socrates says, "At the age of fifty, those who have survived the tests and been successful in practical matters and in the sciences must be led to the goal and compelled to lift up the radiant light of their souls to what itself provides light for everything"—an untenebrous vision of the Form of the Good, Plato's Form of forms. He continues, "They must each in turn put the city, its citizens, and themselves in order, using [the Good] as their model" (540a-b). Overall, the education of the complete guardians is thorough and rigorous. It aims to teach love of toil and truth, selfcontrol, and greatness of soul.

Socrates replies laconically to Adeimantus' challenge, "In crafting our polis, we are not aiming to make any one group of people outstandingly happy, but to make the polis outstandingly happy, inasmuch as that is possible."

---

[3] My translations throughout. Plato, *Republic,* vols. 1 and 2, trans. Paul Shorey (Cambridge: Harvard University Press, [1930] 1994 and [1935] 1987).

[4] Due mostly to high infant-mortality.

The aim for Plato is for a polis to have that functional unity that an organic body possesses. Says Socrates later in the book (462b): "Is there any greater evil for a polis than what rends apart it and makes it many and not one? Is there any greater good than what binds it and makes it one?"

Jefferson's aim is the same—that a state or nation have the greatest possible functional unity. Like Plato, he too distinguishes in a letter to Peter Carr (7 Sept. 1814) between two sorts of citizens—the laborers and the learned. The laborers are to participate at the level of wards (the smallest political units); the learned, in the schools, in the higher levels of government, and in employment, like science, that lends itself readily toward human progress. Over a year later, he writes to Joseph Cabell (2 Feb. 1816) concerning the need of each citizen contributing to the fullest possible extent. "Where every man is a sharer in the direction of his ward republic, or of some of the higher ones, and feels that he is a participator in the government of affairs not merely at an election one day in the year, but every day; when there shall not be a man in the State who will not be a member of some one of it's councils, great or small, he will let the heart be torn out of his body, sooner than his power be wrested from him by a Caesar or a Bonaparte."

In another letter to Joseph C. Cabell (28 Nov. 1820), Jefferson writes of "the greatest good" for any republican government. "That good requires, that while they [the general citizenry] are instructed in general, competently to the common business of life, others should employ their genius with necessary information to the useful arts, to inventions for saving labor and increasing our comforts, to nourishing our health, to civil government, military science, &c." While the general citizenry are to receive a basic education, sufficient to make them self-sufficient in daily affairs, those with greater genius and moral sensitivity are to devote themselves to practical other-regarding tasks. To fulfil such tasks, the most intellectually and morally promising citizens must have access to elite-level education. The notion is starkly Platonic. The elite in a Jeffersonian republic are much like Plato's complete guardians, who in ruling a polis and securing its wellbeing and happiness, are disregarding their own wellbeing and happiness.

For Plato, though each group has its role and each of these roles is critical in the functional wellbeing of a polis, the role of the highest class, the rulers, is most important in allowing for even the possibility of any degree of functional unity in a republic, once the republic is established (494a–b and 499a–d). Thus, for Plato, justice is system-driven, more than people-driven. The system guarantees that there will be virtuous persons and virtuous persons ensure the justice and overall virtue of a polis.

All citizens play an important role, but the system is secured for all intents and purposes from the top-down, because of the virtue of the rulers, and their virtue is guaranteed by their pedigree and education. As Julia Annas writes, "Plato's repeated insistence that the city stands or falls with the Guardians' education, and that the role of laws is fairly minor, plays an important part in the belief that the state and the individual person are analogous in their nature and virtues."[5] Thus, the polis and the human soul are homomorphic. The human soul has an intellective, a courageous, and an appetitive part. It is the same with a polis, with rulers, driven by intellect, guardians, driven by courage, and laborers, driven by appetite.

For Jefferson, the division of the laboring and the learned is not decided by birth or wealth, but by the rise of character and talent through perseverance, labor, and opportunity, seized opportunely. Those persons Jefferson calls in a letter to John Adams (28 Oct. 1813) the "natural aristoi."[6] Like Plato's republic, justice is system-driven in that Jefferson advises that there be tiers of government—wards, counties, states, and the nation[7]—in accordance with the principle that the will of the people decides political issues, and he proposes educational reform to prompt political participation and to function as a check on political corruption. Thus, Jefferson, pace zealous critics like Conor Cruise O'Brien and Michael Hardt,[8] is not a radical or anarchic liberal, whose notion of liberty is exclusively "freedom from." A certain minimal structure, typified by republics within republics and a constitution of constitutions (viz., Bill of Rights),[9] must be in place to ensure responsible and responsive government for the people.

## The Platonic Problem

Given that Jefferson believes the natural *aristoi* are identifiable by both talent and virtue and that morality is foundational for politics—a point that does not escape Merrill Peterson's notice[10]—Jefferson runs into a problem similar to that of Plato—what I call the "problem of Plato's cave."[11] When Adeimantus notes that the structure of the harmonized

---

[5] Julia Annas, *An Introduction to Plato's Republic* (Oxford: Clarendon Press, 1981), 106.
[6] Greek for "best men."
[7] E.g., TJ to Samuel Kercheval, 12 July 1816.
[8] Conor Cruise O'Brien, *The Long Affair: Thomas Jefferson and the French Revolution, 1785-1800* (Chicago: University of Chicago Press, 1996), and Michael Hardt, "Jefferson and Democracy," *American Quarterly*, Vol. 59, 2007, No. 1, 41-78.
[9] See M. Andrew Holowchak, "Individual Liberty and Political Unity in an Expanding Nation: The Axiological Primacy of Wards in Jefferson's Republican Schema," *Thomas Jefferson and Philosophy: Essays on the Philosophical Cast of Jefferson's Writings*, ed. M. Andrew Holowchak (Lanham, MD: Lexington Books, 2014).
[10] Merrill D. Peterson, Thomas Jefferson & the New Nation, 974.
[11] M. Andrew Holowchak, "The Paradox of Public Service: Jefferson, Education, and the Problem of Plato's Cave," *Studies in Philosophy and Education*, Vol. 32, No. 1, 2013, 73-86.

republic that Socrates proposes seems to be such that those responsible for maintaining the unity and harmony, the rulers, would be the least happy, Socrates we recall replies that the aim of a stable, thriving polis is not to make any one group of persons especially happy, but to make the whole as happy as it can be. Socrates subsequently goes on to show that those citizens—with the fullest education and in complete realization that their greatest personal happiness comes in contemplation, not political activity—will recognize the greater good of acting against self-interest and toward the betterment of their polis (514a–518b).

Jefferson faces a similar problem. Like Plato, he notes that those citizens, fittest to govern, are ill disposed to govern, and that those citizens, unfittest to govern, are eager to govern. The persons, large in number, who are willing to assume the most important political stations are not the natural *aristoi*, but the artificial *aristoi*, as their claim to being "best" is meretricious—i.e., it rests merely on birth or wealth. Yet the true *aristoi*, the natural *aristoi*, in possession of virtue and talent, are quick to recognize the entrapments of public office, as it comes at the expenses of personal happiness and of the order of their domestic affairs, and it seemingly offers in return only power and political fame—two "returns" to which a virtuous person is indifferent. "In a virtuous government," writes Jefferson to Richard Henry Lee (17 June 1779), "public offices are, what they should be, burthens to those appointed to them, which it would be wrong to decline, though foreseen to bring with them intense labour, and great private loss."[12] In short, it is difficult to practice politics and sustain virtue, or any sort of progress toward it. Says Jefferson to Jacob van Staphorst (28 Feb. 1790), "After an absence of ten years from my estate I found it much deteriorated & requiring time & advances to bring it back again to the productive state of which it was susceptible."

Why then would any sensible person wish to run for public office? If indifferent to the exercise of power and to fame, what inducements are there for the natural *aristoi*?

Like Plato, Jefferson proffers education as a solution to the difficulty. For Jefferson, higher education with a republican slant is suitably and secularly designed to give scholars fullest appreciation of the gains of liberty and of progress for all citizens and the need of personal sacrifice by the most valuable members of a society to nurture and preserve liberty for the sake of scientific, political, and moral advance. The aim is human flourishing, not self-flourishing. He writes in the "Rockfish Gap Report" (1818):

---

[12] See also TJ to John Randolph, 25 Aug. 1775; TJ to David Rittenhouse, 19 July 1778; TJ to Gen. George Washington, 28 May 1781; TJ to Marquis de Lafayette, 4 Aug. 1781; TJ to Edmund Randolph, 16 Sept. 1781; TJ to Col. James Monroe, 20 May 1782; TJ to John Paradise, 5 July 1789; and TJ to Tho-mas Mann Randolph, 1 Jan. 1792.

Education ... engrafts a new man on the native stock, and improves what in his nature was vicious and perverse into qualities of virtue and social worth. And it cannot be but that each generation succeeding to the knowledge acquired by all those who preceded it, adding to it their own acquisitions and discoveries, and handing the mass down for successive and constant accumulation, must advance the knowledge and well-being of mankind, not infinitely, as some have said, but indefinitely, and to a term which no one can fix and foresee.

Those scholars "graduating" from the University of Virginia, or any other higher-education institution of republican persuasion, will merely recognize their duty, based on a keen and fully developed inner sense of benevolence, to embrace liberty and promote progress, and to act, as philosopher Immanuel Kant would say, not merely consistent with their duty, but in fullest recognition of their duty. Writes Jefferson to George Washington (15 Dec. 1789): "It is not for an individual to choose his post. You are to marshal us as may best be for the public good." Decades later, he says to William Duane (12 Oct. 1812) concerning "the Roman principle," which deems it honorable "for the General of yesterday to act as a Corporal to day if his services can be useful to his country,' for it is "false pride which postpones the public good to any private or personal considerations."

That is consistent with Plato's famed "Allegory of the Cave" in his Republic (514a ff.). A prisoner, having spent his entire life shackled in a Cimmerian cave, once freed from his shackles and able to leave the cave, will leave the cave, see the brilliancy of the sun, and recognize that everything he took to be actual in the cave was part of a world of shadows, not realities. Yet once enlightened, he will willingly return to the cave, even if scorned and chided by those remaining in the cave, to eradicate what darkness he can through efforts to educate his oscitant friends in the cave.

For Jefferson, the scenario is redoubled in perilous times, which call for action. "The times heretofore made it a duty to sacrifice one's wishes to a common cause," says Jefferson, to Colonel John Syne (17 Sept. 1792), concerning the revolutionary years. He then adds, "The duty no longer exists," as the times are no longer perilous.

Jefferson did retire for several years, after serving as Washington's Secretary of State. Nonetheless, events soon beckoned his services. He ran for president in 1796, lost, and assumed the vice-presidency in John Adams' administration. In 1800, he again ran for president, and won. Following Washington's lead, he served two terms—the first marked a period of unexampled American prosperity; the second was marred by threat of war with England.

Yet consistent with the Stoicism he practiced and with his belief that the generations of humans are ever advancing in intellect and moral sensitivity, Jefferson believed that there was a time for governing and there is a time to be governed, a time for fullest activity and a time for diminished activity. He continues in the 1812 letter to William Duane: "I am past service. the hand of age is upon me. the decay of bodily faculties apprises me that those of the mind cannot be unimpaired, had I not still better proofs. every year counts by increased debility, and departing faculties keep the score. the last year it was the sight, this it is the hearing, the next something else will be going, until all is gone." To Henry Dearborn (17 Aug. 1821), he states: "Man, like the fruit he eats, has his period of ripeness. Like that, too, if he continues longer hanging to the stem, it is but an useless and unsightly appendage." To Mrs. Katherine Duane Morgan (26 June 1822), he calls himself a "presque octogenaire," who has been for a long time unfit for political action. Nature herself, over time, "warns us to retire and leave to the generation of the day the direction of its own affairs."

Just 10 days prior to his death, Jefferson writes to Mayor Roger C. Weightman (24 June 1826) in response to a request that he participate in festivities concerning the fiftieth anniversary of the Declaration of Independence. "Acquiescence is a duty, under circumstances not placed among those we are permitted to control." Nevertheless, due to declining health—a situation beyond his control—he declined the invitation. As is well known, he and John Adams died on that memorable day of celebration. It was a fit end for two such American giants.

# Effective History

## The Horizon for Sustained and Catalytic Change at the University of Virginia, Or Why It Was Necessary to Publish *Key to the Door*

Maurice Apprey

> *"In the process of understanding, a real fusing of horizons occurs—which means that as the historical horizon is projected, it is simultaneously superseded. To bring about this fusion in a regulated way is the task of what we call historically effected consciousness."*
> –Hans-Georg Gadamer

WHEN I FIRST JOINED THE FACULTY at the University of Virginia in the early eighties as a professor of Psychiatry in the School of Medicine, the university was a most intellectually rich and vibrant institution. It was the era of Richard Rorty, the well-known philosophical pragmatist, Ralph Cohen, the founding editor of *The New Literary History*, and E.D. Hirsch, an astute champion of authorial intent. Later on I became a senior fellow under Ralph Cohen in the erstwhile Commonwealth Center for Literary and Cultural Change at the University. In that era there were just as many faculty members as students taking or visiting Rorty's class on Heidegger or "From Hegel to Derrida." I was a psychoanalyst and a student of Continental philosophy, specifically in the constitutive tradition of Edmund Husserl, the father of phenomenology, the praxis of pure description. Nevertheless, I spent many lunch hours sitting in on Rorty's lectures.

In one lecture, Rorty reveled in identifying some of his favorite Cartesian splits: meaning and significance; essence and accidents; the real X and the ostensible X; intrinsic and extrinsic; and so on. Ever the philosophical pragmatist, he clearly had no patience for dichotomous thinking.

Similarly inclined, I argue that an account of a historical event at the University of Virginia, a University founded by Thomas Jefferson, would benefit more from a mediating position than a dichotomous stance. Accordingly, I want to take a hint from Hans-Georg

Gadamer in order to situate myself between two horizons in the first instance and then interrogate the effects of history on a contemporary issue—namely, life at the University of Virginia for its early African American-graduates. This was ostensibly the reason for asking for a grant from The Jefferson Trust, an initiative of the University of Virginia Alumni Association, to publish the book, *Key to the Door*.

My pretext then is the following: It is possible to pay homage to the early African-American graduates and still affirm the positive changes taking place at a university, founded by a gentleman who owned slaves. I shall use as my text for this inquiry the book I co-edited with Shelli Poe, *The Key to the Door: Experiences of Early African-American Students at the University of Virginia*.[1] The context is my discovery that I am uncannily in the very stories I want to tell about our early graduates from the University, and yet the stories are essentially not about me. The stories are largely about these early graduates who largely endured hardship and still stayed and graduated.

## Conceptual Prejudgments

In order to nuance my argument for publishing the book, I turn to the philosopher Hans-Georg Gadamer's *Truth and Method* (1960) for the conceptual presence that I bring to the book. A number of questions arose for me. What constitutes historical interest? What is the effect of history? What is the imperative to grasp effective history? Within whose horizon can a story be told? How does a transposition from one horizon to another take place? What is the place of complementarity, of reciprocity of horizons? Most importantly, how does one who wants to understand history and its effect participate in a fusion of horizons without resolving that tension between them?

Gadamer in *Truth and Method* provides one direction for getting a handle on these questions. For him historical interest is directed toward historical phenomena and traditional work as well as their *effect in history*. Privileging the effect in history, making the implicit become explicit became a new demand. Why? For him that explicitation [sic] became peremptory because "we are always *already* affected by history"[2] (emphasis added). There is the additional imperative to understand ourselves better and to grasp that in all understanding the efficacy of history is at work. Gadamer saw the imperative to grasp effective history as necessary for fostering scientific consciousness. Consciousness of being affected

---

[1] Maurice Apprey and Shelli Poe, *The Key to the Door: Experiences of the Early Students at the University of Virginia* (Charlottesville: University of Virginia Press, 2017).
[2] Hans-Georg Gadamer, *Truth and Method* (New York: Continuum Press, 1975), 300.

by history is primarily consciousness of the hermeneutic situation. In this respect, we are never in some ek-static position of standing outside history; rather, we are in it. The illumination is not finite or complete.

Our knowledge of ourselves being essentially incomplete, we need an appropriate historical horizon in order to grasp the dimensions of the historical object to be understood. By horizon Gadamer wished to expand the superior breath of vision that a subject must have in order to understand a phenomenon beyond what is close at hand. Openness is needed to foster an imaginative projection into a past or into a new present and into another human life. The means that coming to grips with that historical object is a *transposition* of ourselves in the position of the other in order to foster understanding. Gadamer says, "We must always *already* have a horizon in order to transpose ourselves into a situation"[3] (emphasis added). *We advance this transposition by rising to a higher universality, and to overcome both our own particularity and the particularity of the other.* When we rise to this superior vision, we acquire a larger perspective and a more authentic proportionality of the historical object.

In addition to the perspectival expansion, something else happens. We foreground the historical object. In so doing, what is foregrounded makes *more visible* that from which that something is foregrounded. Then we test our prejudices and do so continually so that old and new perspectives combine into "something of living value without either being expressly foregrounded from the other."[4]

In the process of understanding then, following Gadamer, "a real fusing of horizons occurs—which means that as the historical horizon is projected, it is simultaneously superseded. To bring about this fusion in a regulated way is the task of what we call historically effected consciousness."[5]

So, I am in the stories of the early black students at the University of Virginia, even as I consciously know that the stories are not essentially about me. I can transpose myself into their stories in ways that surrender the particularity of my horizon and that of the authors' historical horizon in order to arrive at a superior vision. One such conceivable superior vision is this: The earliest African-American students to matriculate at the University of Virginia had to surrender the particularity of their private pain and suffering in order to reach the summit of their educational aspirations—a summit that links up with Thomas Jefferson's catalytic impulse to create a national university.[6]

---

[3] Hans-Georg Gadamer, *Truth and Method*, 305.
[4] Hans-Georg Gadamer, *Truth and Method*, 306.
[5] Hans-Georg Gadamer, *Truth and Method*, 307.
[6] Alfred J. Mapp, *Thomas Jefferson: Passionate Pilgrim* (Lanham, MD: Rowman & Littlefield, 1991).

## Textual Constitution

The title of *The Key to the Door* was taken from a story told by one of the early graduates who was so terrified on his first day that he inadvertently left the key to his door in the outside lock. White-American students banged at his door in protest all night. The next day he discovered that the key to his room had been left in the outside lock and so students could easily have walked in. The title is also a metaphor. The early graduates suffered in the process of integrating the University of Virginia. Their suffering and successes opened the door for future students like them to matriculate at the University. As a cautionary tale, the key that opens the door can lock it. This means that the University cannot become complacent, and happily, the University has made exponential gains in the quality of student life and academic achievements. As one White-American alumnus put it in a private conversation: "The University was good when I was here. It is a great University now that women and Africa-Americans are here."

*The Key to the Door* begins with an archivist's account of history of the early years from segregation to desegregation, continues with representative accounts of the experiences of the early graduates and ends with representative achievements and some limits of the University as it stands today.

Revisiting the fusion of horizons between the experiences of the early graduates and my own as a Professor of Psychiatry and as a young Assistant dean of students in the early 1980s, I see a number of connections. Their task was to study under unfavorable conditions and still graduate. My job as Assistant Dean of students was to recruit, retain, and graduate students in the medical school in greater numbers.

A vignette would tell us a great deal about the conditions of the time. It was 1983. I had just received a federal grant to create an academic support program that included a six-week summer retention program. It was a program that was a mini-medical school, as it were. I needed five professors to teach a hybrid chemistry course that taught students ahead of time many essential physico-chemical principles they would need upon matriculation into medical school. I needed a second professor to teach the essential quantitative and statistical skills they would need in medical school. After the physico-chemical skills and the quantitative segments, the students would take sections of medical-school courses in biochemistry, physiology and genetics. All these were suitably arranged without a hitch.

Then came the anatomy portion of the summer program. No University of Virginia faculty would teach it. I had to secure an instructor from outside the University. I found one that was a physician and Ph.D. graduate in Anatomy from Cambridge University in England. Even so the Department would not let him teach dissection in their laboratory until the Medical School dean overrode the faculty.

Finally, the dean asked me to visit three department chairs to get sufficient buy-in before the program could begin. One department chair was uninterested and wondered why I had been asked to confer with him. A second chair was interested but did not have time to meet with me. A third violently swore at me. "What the f*** do you think you are doing creating such a difficult program for students who are totally underprepared for medical school?" I calmly responded, "Sir, rumor has it that if the program were not rigorous enough, you will be the first to call it a Mickey Mouse program." He softened his tone and offered to make the program both rigorous and "fun" for the students.

For over 20 years, this remarkable physician created exposures to clinical medicine for our UVA premedical students on a daily basis. He mentored new matriculants into the School of Medicine and sponsored many African-American students for first-rate post-graduate residencies. He became the co-investigator of grants, helped us secure at least 10,000,000 dollars in sponsored awards before he died in his hotel room outside Philadelphia while he was on his way to secure more grants for the program.

After 36 years, the program has outlived its purpose and our students are now recipients of multiple national awards and accolades.

The story of student academic support at the University of Virginia, in my view, is a quintessentially Jeffersonian story. Who would have thought that a University that once paid the tuition of African-American students to study at Columbia University and others would have the highest ranking graduation rate among its peer state-supported institutions?

A Ghanaian, a clinician trained by Anna Freud as a psychoanalyst in London, is thrown into an administrative role to recruit, retain, and graduate underrepresented and under-served students, mostly African-Americans.

As an educator, he created facilitating entry, retention and graduation programs at the School of Medicine and in the College of Liberal Arts and Sciences. As a Husserlian phenomenologist, he kept constituting and reconstituting his understanding of what he had been thrown into. As a psychoanalyst he knew from his training that he was in the story and the story needed not to be about him. Thirty seven years later, the fruition of fusing the horizons of his students, young and old, with his own multidimensional and multidisciplinary heritage came together to arrive at a place we can call both Gadamerian and Jeffersonian in the sense that my particularity and the particularity of my students have been overcome in order to arrive at a higher vision and outcome.

Henceforth, the University of Virginia will not be the same place it once was, especially in the 1950s and 1960s, when new African-American students began to matriculate. Now Thomas Jefferson's Academical Village is a paradigm for catalytic excellence.

# Thomas Jefferson
# University Founder and Virginia Rebel

William Wilson

IT TAKES A LIFETIME OF STUDY TO BEGIN to understand the variegated mind of Thomas Jefferson, and one of the greatest mistakes one can make along the way—one in no way reserved for the novice—is to split the Virginia rebel apart from the scholar of immense learning. We often begin study of the third president with a preconceived notion that any fiery politician who could overturn the established order could not also be the leading scholar *of* that order; and then we simply admit that he was a man of two disparate and immense talents and vocations, and throw up our hands at the "complexity."

In all fairness, Jefferson himself leads us into this error by saying throughout his life that he longed for the day when he could retire from public life and return to his books (and gardens and fields) at Monticello, thereby separating service and scholarship. But we see clearly throughout this public life—from his days as a young Virginia Burgess to his second term as President of the United States—that he was always pursuing the Classics (in Latin and Greek), contemporary science, philosophy, history, and much else, with the energy and excellence of a great professor. His hopes of returning to Albemarle were simply wishes to return home. There were never these two sides to Jefferson. Scholarship was not for Jefferson "part and parcel" with public service, and vise-versa. For him, the two activities were one, and which he performed for one reason—republican liberty.

Jefferson never believed that his retirement would be that of a scholarly recluse, free of the alarms and distresses that accompanied the making and preserving of the American Republic. Five years after leaving the presidency, he wrote to the Marquis de Lafayette (14 Feb. 1815) about a lesson he learned well as an early observer of the French Revolution. He said that there is a "mortifying alternative" now being handed the "French Patriot," of either "remaining silent, or disgraced ... by "Bonapartism." This sad choice, he went on to say, is the result of French liberty "recovered by force, and placed on the backs of an unprepared people." Tyranny can result from this republican unpreparedness as much as it did not too long ago by the now defeated monarchy. This analysis of forlorn France, Jefferson argues, can be equally applied to the United States. "The Marats, the Dantons, and the Robespierres, of Massachusetts are in the same pay, under the same orders and making the same efforts to anarchize us, that their prototypes in France did there. Jefferson's remedy for both countries—not advice, but remedy, if we read the letter carefully—is an educated wisdom, or what he often simply called "science." Both countries must come under the hand of "reasonable laws favoring the progress of knowledge in the general mass of the people, and a liberty which takes root and growth in the progress of reason."

This is a striking piece of correspondence concerning two desperate political crises. There is no mention of political maneuvers or tactics—no watch-and-wait policies. There is just one "fix," one remedy. He and the marquis must educate the general "masses." Doing so would prepare for and secure liberty.

Five years later the Marats, the Dantons, and the Robespierres of New England, for Jefferson, took a second turn at political turmoil by being the signal cause of the Missouri Comprise, that "fire bell in the night," as he put it, which he said left him at the time in no doubt that it was the Union's knell. On April 22, 1820, he wrote to John Holmes, "I regret that I am to die in the belief that the useless sacrifice of themselves by the generation of '76 to acquire self government and happiness to their country is to be thrown away by the unwise and unworthy passions of their sons, and that my only consolation is to be that I live not to weep over it."[1]

Though he was in despair, this gloomy thought remained but a "belief," (as we see above). There was no resignation on his part. Nor was there merely a rallying of the Republicans to combat the New England Federalists. His hopes remained strong, and the battle would be waged against all monopolies of power by education. The dream of his last years was to design, build, and fund a great university. The cornerstone had been laid, and the Virginia legislature had approved the curriculum, location, and funding—all under the leadership of Jefferson, if not in several instances, by his single hand. Only the students were needed. It was here in the University of Virginia that he laid his hopes.

Hardly a retirement "project," as many today would call or consider it, the university was to be the source of that indispensable learning which is not simply a requirement for a nation to become and remain a civil society, but one which has the acuity to see the face of tyranny in all of its protean and masked forms. As Jefferson wrote to John Tyler (26 May, 1810), "The main purpose of the institution is for the student to judge for himself what will secure or endanger his freedom."

---

[1] The Compromise allowed Missouri to enter the Union as a slave state but with the provision that slavery would be illegal above the line 36°30'. Jefferson thought that this geographical line splitting apart current and future states, and hardened by irreconcilable political differences, was irreparable.

Accordingly Jefferson wanted a university that would be "broad," "liberal," and not "two centuries out of date" as he believed were true of Oxford, Cambridge, and Sorbonne. An up-to-date university for modern administrators is one that offers courses matching the current needs of the job market, or talents ill-defined and standing alone such as "leadership." He, of course, wanted students to be able to take a part in current affairs and to satisfy the current needs of the nation. But the purpose of the university was to graduate students with the "cut" of mind to recognize and isolate the "rub" of traditional truths, and then act not in the ways that mistook the traditional for the habitual or conventional, but rather saw in them a revolutionary edict that was absolutely incumbent. The Jesus of the Bible Jefferson edited for his own devotion said that the poor are blessed and honored by God. Thus they are not simply to be clothed and fed but also to be exalted among us.

An excellent example of what Jefferson wanted out of university education is found in a letter he wrote to John Adam's son in law, W.S. Smith (13 Nov. 1787). Young Smith was deeply troubled by the current rebellions in New England and felt that they demonstrated an unbridled addiction to raw power, and especially in their representatives in the Federal government. Jefferson agreed with this assessment, but was unmoved and quieted Smith's alarm, but he does so with a lesson more troubling than the report of New England violence. "The tree of liberty must be refreshed from time to time with the blood of patriots and tyrants. It is its natural manure." He makes this startling, familiar, and troubling rejoinder because for him rebellions are always great reminders to government authorities that the people are awake and watching. Thus, "God forbid that we should ever be twenty years without such a rebellion." If the rebels are in the wrong they can be corrected, and being rebellious and wrong is better than the "lethargy" that brings about the death of republics.

Dumas Malone in his celebrated biography of Jefferson said that if you want to know Jefferson the radical do not look at the tree-of-liberty passage. Instead, look again at the Declaration of Independence.[2] Exactly. In the Declaration one sees the stark, and to many still today, the outrageous point about the inevitability of rebellion. These violent outbursts are inevitable because quite simply no government is sovereign. Only the people are sovereign, and therefore the people must cashier the government when it turns tyrannical, which at some point, given human nature, is bound to occur. What was happening in New England, however violent and fearsome, was simply an example of the constant strife between those with rights to power (the people) and the great pretender (their government).

---

[2] Dumas Malone, *Jefferson and His Time, Vol. II. Jefferson and the Rights of Man* (Boston: Little Brown and Co.), 165-166.

People will always rebel when their rights are threatened, whether rightly or wrongly; there is nothing new in that. But the true enemy of government, the constant revolutionary, is the one who wrote the Declaration, the one who is pleased to know that the spirit of 1776, whether ill-advised or not, is alive and well. Error can be corrected. Lethargy kills.

Though Jefferson's mind delved into all of the many things he found interesting and made hundreds of recordings and reports about them, his mind was not complex. One of his three heroes in the Enlightenment was Sir Isaac Newton who threw out centuries of what really for Jefferson was complex and extremely puzzling—old and reigning Aristotelian metaphysics—simply to observe nature with new eyes and then record what he saw. Jefferson was quite Newtonian when his close observations of historical order and disorder enabled him to locate a novel form of tyranny arising in the French Republic. Accordingly, he warned Lafayette. He had learned to see through what was merely standard in rebellions—the winners and losers, the torture, the hilarity, and the wretchedness—to witness the unique shape of power that at this moment threatens. We suffer a deadly type of ignorance if we do not have this ability. Thus, he tells Lafayette to educate the masses. Policy, tactics, and maneuvers will surely fail in a horrific blood-bath if they rest on ignorance. Also, to be such an astute observer of political order and disorder is to have learned the truth of the Declaration, or to be well on the way to learning it.

Another illustration of Jefferson's unique and radical views on learning is found in his Bill for the More General Diffusion of Knowledge that he submitted in 1778 to the Virginia legislature—a body of men that often balked at the price of, and doubted the need for, state-sponsored learning. In this situation we would expect anyone, and especially one with Jefferson's eloquence, to take on the role of a pitchmen. But Jefferson declined the role. He not only argued in this document that education is required for a free republic, he went further and asserted that combating despotism is the sole reason for having a learned citizenry. He offered no other argument at all.

> Experience hath shown that even under the best forms (of government), those entrusted with power have, in time, and by slow operations, perverted into tyranny; and it is believed that the most effectual means of preventing this would be, to illuminate, as far as practicable, the minds of the people at large, and more especially to give them knowledge of those facts, which history exhibiteth, that, possessed thereby of the experience of other ages and countries, they may be enabled to know ambition under all its shapes, and prompt to exert their natural powers to defeat its purposes.... Thus it becomes expedient for promoting the public happiness that ... liberal education ... render those persons able to guard the sacred deposits of the rights and liberties of their fellow citizens.

Jefferson devoted several pages of the bill to a presentation of a state-wide program for elementary, secondary, and university education, but his case for Virginia needing education at all is only about one fifth of the entire document. Education, as we see in the quotation above, is needed to "guard the sacred deposits of the rights and liberties" of the people. What more needs to be said? What other reason is there?

Jefferson repeats and extends this same case in his Bill for Establishing Religious Freedom (1779, passed in 1786). Here not only does he argue that education is the only safeguard against tyranny, he then turns the case around to show that the essence of tyranny, no matter what form it takes in history, is a crime that *fundamentally* intends the destruction of free minds. In other words, education is not simply the only safeguard against despotism. Tyranny destroys civic order by taking aim specifically at the intellect.

> Well aware of the opinions and beliefs of men depend not only on their own will, but follow involuntarily the evidence proposed to their minds; that Almighty God hath created the mind free, and manifested his supreme will that free it shall remain by making it altogether insusceptible of restraint; that all attempts to influence it by temporal punishments, or burthens, or by civil incapacitations, tend only to beget habits of meanness and hypocrisy.

He continues, "Impious ... legislators and rulers, civil as well as ecclesiastical ... have assumed dominion over the faith of others ... and as such endeavoring to impose their own opinions and modes of thinking."

Thus, the very nature of tyranny is to "*compel* a man to accept opinions he both disbelieves and abhors." Whereas the mind can only be compelled by evidence it takes to be evidentially persuasive.

In other words, all of the historical crimes of the despot to persuade—torture, lies, flattery, and bribes among others—for Jefferson, can all be reduced to the absurd and diabolical attempt to force beliefs on a mind created free. Should the tyrant boast that he or she has in fact changed opinions down through the ages, the educated person will say: "Think again. You have compelled nothing. But you have destroyed a mind." The mind is moved by evidentially persuasive evidence and nothing else.

When Jefferson wrote to William Roscoe (27 Dec. 1820) the famous words that "here (at the University of Virginia) we are not afraid to follow truth wherever it may lead, nor to tolerate any error so long as reason is left free to combat it," he was describing the proper functioning of free minds, and he penned these words in direct reference to current political turmoil in England—specifically to the tyranny of King George III, the enemy of the

American Revolution. He was not, that is, seeking ornamental language to be carved onto university buildings.[3]

In his Report of the Commissioners for the University of Virginia (4 Aug. 1818), Jefferson spoke in general terms of the common good of learning, such as it "develops reasoning faculties," "habits of reflection," "love of virtue," and "indefinite improvement." But once again, the purpose is to ready defenders of liberty against the "alliance of church and state" and its ... monopolies of power." No other goal is mentioned.

The report lists 10 schools,[4] and so devoted was Jefferson to the freedom of the mind that he insisted that UVa's students would be allowed to choose their own classes, a privilege unheard of in universities of his time. The field of divinity is notoriously missing from the list. The sole purpose of many American universities was to ensure the training of clergy, and the field was required of all students. In the 1818 report, Jefferson said his reasons for the omission were in "conformity with the principles of our Constitution ... that all sects of religion are on an equal footing."

There was more to his omission of a professorship of Divinity than this, however. We have seen that he wanted the church separated from the state in order to keep the hands of government off the private faith of the people. He emphatically did not want this separation, as so many Americans today think in some perverse inclination to misread him, to enable government to protect people from unwanted intrusions of religion. Given what we have seen him say about government in this essay, it is unthinkable that he would trust it with this rare privilege and extreme power.

Jefferson was never "anti-religion." His harsh words for much of orthodox Christianity—such as taking the doctrine of the Trinity to be an absurdity or the divinity of Christ an invention of priests to lure credulous souls into their sway—he said in *defense* of religion because he thought that doctrines such as these were signs that a true faith had been corrupted by monopolies of power in church and state. This true religion was to be sought by every person individually through a soul-searching and critical investigation of evidence and conscience. And he advised and counseled this spiritual trial for the exact same reasons he boasted that at the University of Virginia "we are not afraid to follow the truth wherever it may lead" so long as reason is ready to combat error.

---

[3] As they are now on the Senff Gate at the UVa.
[4] Ancient Languages, Modern Languages, Mathematics, Physico-Mathematics (meaning applied mathematics), Physics or Natural Philosophy, Botany-Zoology, Anatomy-Medicine, Government, Law, and Ideology (meaning Grammar, Ethics, Rhetoric, Belle Lettres, and Fine Arts.

For instance, from Paris he wrote to his nephew Peter Carr (10 Aug. 1787) that Carr must examine thus his own beliefs. "Divest yourself of all bias in favor of novelty & singularity of opinion." Religion, he said, is "too important" for such frivolity "and the consequences may be too serious." His nephew was bravely to "shake off all fears and servile prejudices ... and "fix reason firmly in her seat, and call to her tribunal every fact, every opinion." Jefferson bid his nephew to "question with boldness even the existence of God." Carr was to read the Bible as he would any ancient text of his heritage, such as Livy and Tacitus, and to be careful to examine all testimonies of miracles because such testimonies are "entitled to your inquiry."

Thus, the discipline of education and the discipline of propounding religious beliefs are one and the same. Both are to prepare the mind to see through error and the corruption of concentrated power. The "love of virtue" and the "habits of reflection" he advertised in his Commissioners' Report, exercised and won through a fearless journey "wherever truth may lead," were to be performed by way of his curriculum of 10 departments. The student's faith is left to take a personal, but similar, pilgrimage.

Any aspect of religion that does invite a rigorous academic investigation—such as whether God can be known through nature or whether a moral life requires faith—Jefferson said would be undertaken in courses through the professorship of ethics. Also, the study of ancient languages would introduce the student to Classical literature as well as important texts in the Jewish and Christian traditions. Furthermore, he hoped that the various denominations would build places of worship and seminaries on the periphery of the Grounds, and that their students would attend classes at the university as well as at the places where they worshiped and prepared for ordination.[5]

To sum up these brief remarks on Thomas Jefferson's thoughts on education we should return to the point made earlier that tyranny is first, foremost, and always a direct attack on the freedom of the mind (and thereby on social order). The tyrant, ignorant of his or her true motives, simply intends to wield unwarranted power for his own gain. But being ignorant, he cannot draw the logical inference that the destruction of freedom is the destruction of mind. He instead aims to oppress the mind—to take away its freedom—and then asks it to give its assent to the emperor's decrees and bidding. No other explanation can explain Jefferson's consistent remarks and presuppositions that the only thing that stands between despotism and the people is education. And we should now see that these

---

[5] Many historians argue that he proposed the ethics courses in natural religion and the seminaries circling the Grounds to placate his critics' charges that he was setting up an atheistic institution. There is no reason to doubt that he hoped both proposals would help pass the report, but there is equally no reason to think that they were merely a ploy.

intellectual journeys—of "truth wherever it may lead," with reason combatting error, and carried out in university exercises as well as in solitary quests for a true faith—are the first footfalls of the freedom he hoped to instill and protect.

This constant bloody exchange between mind and raw power is best seen in the turmoil in Jefferson's mind over slavery. For he said in his only book, *Notes on the State of Virginia* (1787), that the "whole commerce between master and slave is … the most unremitting despotism" against the free mind which "is the gift of God."[6] The right to exercise this freedom (and thereby to "dissolve political bands") is "self-evident," as the Congressional Committee for the Declaration of Independence put it. It is "inherent" as Jefferson's own draft said before the Committee altered his words.

Accordingly, five years later in the *Notes on the State of Virginia*, Jefferson held that abolishing the despicable institution of slavery is a subject "about which it is impossible to be temperate." That is, it is not a matter to be settled "by various considerations of policy, of morals, of history natural and civil." For how can policy considerations, moral theorizing, and any kind of historical study *make* acceptable what is already "self-evident," "inherent," and thus by logic, required? One must be "contented to hope" that the truth will "force its way into everyone's mind."[7] It is well worth considering whether Jefferson gave up on his own policy of slow emancipation, training, and colonization for just these reasons. In his last year he said, "My sentiments have been 40 years before the public. Had I repeated them 40 times, they would only have become the more stale and threadbare."[8] For it was not a policy that was "threadbare."

Jefferson left abolition and the securing of racial justice to future generations along with great thoughts and institutions where the freedom of the mind could be exercised and, with hope, become virtuous. There certainly remain many errors to combat.

---

[6] Thomas Jefferson, *Notes on the State of Virginia*, in *Thomas Jefferson, Writings*, ed. Merrill D. Peterson (New York: Library of America, 1984), 288.
[7] Thomas Jefferson, *Notes on the State of Virginia*, 289.
[8] TJ to James Heaton, 20 May 1826.

# Thomas Jefferson's Conception of "Academic Freedom" and Its Current Condition in American Higher Education

Garrett Ward Sheldon

*"Here we are not afraid to follow the truth wherever it may lead, nor to tolerate any error, so long as reason is left free to combat it."*
–Thomas Jefferson

THOMAS JEFFERSON'S CONCEPTION OF "Academic Freedom" became the standard of modern intellectual progress in America and the world. Its components of both individual freedom of inquiry in expression and debate along with lively, free and tolerant academic community were seen as essential to all other forms of progress: political, economic, social and ethical.

This Jeffersonian ideal of Academic Freedom in the university and all its positive effects on the rest of American Society has come under assault throughout history from religious bigotry, social intolerance, and political ideology, most recently from the federal government's expansion of the Title IX law during the past six years. It almost destroyed university knowledge and learning, the lively academic community as well as their attendant social and personal benefits.

## Individual Expression in an Academic Community

Jefferson's conception of Academic Freedom within the University of Virginia contained both a component of individual freedom to inquire into, express, and debate all manner of thoughts and ideas, and an academic environment conducive to such intellectual activity in a lively, tolerant, confident, and pleasant community. It is no coincidence that Jefferson referred to the University of Virginia as an "Academic Village." True learning, knowledge, truth, and education as well as discovering new meaning and developing thinking and human reasoning abilities require both individual liberty to pursue knowledge and a collegial environment that encourages and rewards such intellectual pursuits. Both the individual mind and the creative society will benefit from such academic freedom. It requires an open, free atmosphere for the expression of all perspectives: questioning, discussion, debate, and ongoing learning. A free and open atmosphere leads to the development of individual abilities, creativity, and happiness as well as advances in science, technology, economics, politics, and ethics. The intellectual progress of the University of Virginia for Jefferson was the engine behind American democracy and freedom.[1]

This perspective goes back to Jefferson's knowledge of classical western philosophy. Jefferson drew inspiration from the Ancient Greek saw, "Know thyself," etched on the wall of the Oracle at Delphi, Socrates' quote in Plato's *Apology*, "the unexamined life is not worth living,"[2] and Aristotle's insistence that every person is a social animal (*politikon zōon*),[3] whose proper end is achieved through "reasoned speech" and "moral choice." Jefferson saw intellectual freedom and growth through reasoned discussion and discovery as the fulfillment of that highest human, rational nature, as well as the development of the most humane, prosperous, and happy society.

Prior to "Mr. Jefferson's University", most American colleges were tied to a religious denomination restricting areas of inquiry and discoveries. Like the recent Title IX restrictions on certain words or subjects, this limited the intellectual life and stifled individual and social development. Instead of a lively, fun atmosphere, there existed a closed, suspicious and fearful environment, hardly conducive to education. Even in the old universities of England—e.g., Oxford and Cambridge, upon which many American colleges were modeled, with their Socratic "tutorials" of pupils presenting arguments to their teachers and defending them from questions and objections—many areas of religious and political information were "off limits." They were simply not discussed because they were heretical, dangerous, and subversive; punishable, if expressed or entertained.

For Jeffersonian higher education, the answer to such "bad" ideas was not suppression and censorship, but their refutation by better ideas, found through good, reasonable argument. As he wrote in defense of religious liberty, "Truth is the proper and sufficient antagonist to error, and has nothing to fear from the conflict, unless, by human interposition, disarmed of her natural weapons, free argument and debate, errors ceasing to be dangerous when it is permitted freely to confront them."[4] Jefferson's declaration of free speech broke

---

[1] See Garrett Ward Sheldon "The Myth of Jefferson's Polysemous Conception of Liberty," in *Thomas Jefferson: The Man behind the Myths*, ed. M. Andrew Holowchak (Jefferson, NC: McFarland, 2017).
[2] Plato, *Apology*, trans. G.M.A. Grube (Indianapolis: Hackett Publishing, 1981), 38a.
[3] Aristotle, *Nicomachean Ethics*, 1097b12 and 1169b19, and *Politics*, 1253a3-4 and 1278b20.
[4] Thomas Jefferson, *The Writings of Thomas Jefferson*, vol. 8, ed. Albert Ellery Bergh (Washington, D.C.: Thomas Jefferson's Memorial Association, 1904-5), 455.

with centuries of restrictions of the mind and discourse in higher education. It saw open discussion, aimed at truth by clashing with and defeating error, as the best means to knowledge, progress, and justice. As Jefferson said to John Adams (1 Aug. 1816): "Bigotry is the disease of ignorance.... Education and free discussion are the antidotes." Applying this "free marketplace of ideas" to the University of Virginia, its founder wrote to William Roscoe (27 Dec. 1820), "This institution will be based on the illimitable freedom of the human mind, [for] here we are not afraid to follow truth wherever it may lead, nor to tolerate any error so long as reason is left free to combat it." Debating all sides of an issue would "distill" the truth (or as much as we can know of it) and ready the mind to approach all new problems and situations.

Professors were to embody that liberal, tolerant approach by encouraging students to examine all ideas in a detached, objective way. Elevating reason over emotion, as the British philosopher John Stuart Mill later wrote in his classic defense of intellectual freedom, *On Liberty*, the liberally educated person would welcome hearing views contrary to his own, and in their most persuasive form, because they would either convert him to a better, more sustainable view, or strengthen his existing view by recognition of their errors. Such free debate requires, besides reasoning skills, humility, for stubborn intolerance and oppression and usually borne of arrogant, unbudging pride. Such free debate also requires an attitude of Socratic "wisdom"—that is, knowing that one does not know,[5] and therefore, humbly seeking the truth. This is not weakness or inferiority, but strength and confidence. Jefferson wanted an American republic full of such strong, confident citizens, so intellectually prepared that they could debate any topic, to the benefit of the best policies, the most just society, and happy and thriving individuals. Only a tyrannical state, with weak and ignorant rulers, would deny such freedom of speech and enforce censorship to stunt economic, political, and social progress.

The sort of academic freedom Jefferson envisaged at the University of Virginia was crucial to his conception of progressive, useful education and a thriving democracy, because it would train leaders in liberal values—justice, freedom, moral sensitivity, and worthwhile industry—and set a global example for other institutions. A rigid, cold, harsh regime—whether Nazi Germany or Soviet Communism of the past, or today the American Title IX bureaucracy, which rules with censorship and fear, spying, interrogation, and persecution of "forbidden" ideas—invariably produces the most narrow and vicious leaders and frightened, ignorant masses.

---

[5] In *Apology*, Socrates admits to a sort of "human wisdom," which is recognition and admission of the "worthless" of human wisdom, next to divine wisdom, 23a-b.

A free, open, and intelligent atmosphere of a true university, for Jefferson, produced the liveliest, happiest, and most rewarding society. At William and Mary College, which Jefferson attended in the mid-1700s, and when being tutored thereafter in law by George Wythe, he enjoyed an educational community that informed his ideals for the University of Virginia's "Academical Village."

Jefferson recognized that individual intellectual growth and development require many informal unofficial societies and relationships in the university "grounds" besides formal classrooms, laboratories, and libraries—hence his notion of an "Academical Village." The common areas of The Lawn, benches, the lake, dining clubs, and friendships are all an integral part of the academic community. Restrictive control over informal settings and relationships stifle learning. Jefferson experienced this positive aspect of college life and attributed much of his learning and accomplishments to it. Such casual, personal social life is one of the most important and pleasant aspects of university life. The radically expanded and rigid Title IX enforcement of these past years in American higher education damages this vital aspect of collegiate life almost as much as its destruction of free speech.

But Jefferson enjoyed both a stimulating, wide-ranging intellectual life *and* a fulfilling informal social life at William and Mary College—both affecting positively his future life and career.

In his *Autobiography*, Jefferson wrote of the influence of William Small on his life. "It was my good fortune, and what probably fixed the destinies of my life, that Dr. William Small of Scotland was then the professor of Mathematics, a man profound in most of the useful branches of science, with a happy talent for communication, correct and gentlemanly manners, and an enlarged and liberal mind."[6] From this gifted professor, Jefferson first experienced the intellectual excitement and joy of lively learning and discussion. Small was not merely an instructor, but also a mentor and friend. Jefferson wrote that Professor Small was his "daily companion," and their "conversation" covered the whole range of knowledge: science, philosophy, ethics, rhetoric and "belles letters" (literature). This also led to Jefferson's introduction to his law professor, George Wythe, who similarly taught legal practice and doctrine within a framework of a liberal education: history, literature, and political philosophy.[7] This way of studying English Common Law greatly affected the arguments and history that informed Jefferson's writings during the American Revolution and in early American Republic.

---

[6] Thomas Jefferson, *Autobiography, Thomas Jefferson: Writings*, ed. Merrill D. Peterson (New York: Library of America, 1984), 4.

[7] Thomas Jefferson, *Autobiography*, 4–5.

Besides this formal education, professors Small and Wythe also introduced Jefferson to the British Royal Governor Francis Fauquier, and Small and Wythe, the four formed a "partie quarree: at dinner parties at the Governor's Palace in Williamsburg. The lively dinner conversations at these social occasions further taught Jefferson the arts of bonhomie and intelligent and pleasant conversation on a whole range of subjects with friends and colleagues. Fauquier was described as "elegant, urbane, learned and witty." He patronized the arts and music, classical concerts, and discussions of French philosophy and literature, and had gentlemanly "taste, refinement and erudition."[8] Thus, Jefferson described his dinner engagements in Williamsburg as "the finest school of manners and morals that ever existed in America."[9] This model of a civilized, lively academic environment birthed Jefferson's idea of the University of Virginia—"this institution will be based on the illimitable freedom of the human mind [for] here we are not afraid to follow truth wherever it may lead, nor to tolerate any error so long as reason is left free to combat it"—which he founded 40 years later. This ethic of free inquiry into all manner of ideas, and of examining all perspectives without fear of offense, became the American ideal of "academic freedom" and of intellectual progress in the United States and in the world, as well as the social mileau of the academy.

So, university education for Jefferson entailed formal and rigorous, yet free and open inquiry, and discussion and debates of all sides of issues in the classroom as well as lectures, seminars, and labs, and the informal unstructured social life of his "Academical Village." There was to be talk, argument, and laughter at meals, on walks, in dorms, on benches, on The Lawn, at theatrical and musical performances, and even before or after chapel. Much of the intellectual and social development was to occur in this community, as it did for Jefferson in Williamsburg.

The benefits of this casual, friendly academic society are equally as important as all the class work, studies, paper, assignments, and presentations. Together, the formal, technical, and informal personal aspects of the University of Virginia would develop the mind, manner, and character of its students and prepared them for life, professional and personal. This strictly academic and indirectly academic atmosphere would provide mentoring and "apprenticeships" that went beyond purely academic learning.

As Jefferson gratefully acknowledged, this combination of the formal and informal atmosphere in his college life prepared him for his extraordinary life achievements. That remains the implicit ethos and goal of American higher education.

---

[8] Merrell Peterson, *Thomas Jefferson and the New Nation* (New York: Oxford University Press, 1970), 14–15.
[9] Thomas Jefferson, *Autobiography*, 4.

Unfortunately, throughout American history and especially in recent years, the rigorous, open, and free academic atmosphere, and the informal social community of the university have been greatly damaged by certain intrusive governmental policies.

## Title IX and the End of Academic Freedom

The Jeffersonian ideal of academic freedom as open, diverse, and rational discussion in a lively, tolerant academic community has been largely destroyed in the past three years by the federal government's (Department of Education, Office of Civil Rights of the Obama Administration) expansion of the Title IX law. This radical, and largely illegal and unconstitutional, expansion of a law designed to maintain gender equality in college sports programs, imposes policies that censor free speech and poisoned the open, positive academic relationships in the academic community. This was done in the name of stopping assault, harassment, and abuse, particularly of women, but it has ended up harming women the most and creating a "hostile environment" for everyone. Fortunately, the Federal Courts reversed dozens of unjust decisions rendered by Title IX officials by tribunals that decided basic due process of law protections. The current administration is undoing much of this bureaucratic overreach. But the damage has been done to American higher education and may take years to repair.

Many books and articles have now been written on this Title IX debacle and its disastrous effects on American Higher Education, but perhaps the best is Laura Kipnis's recent book *Unwanted Advances*. As professor of theater and film at Northwestern University, she has personally experienced a Title IX "Inquisition" and has heard from hundreds of faculty who underwent similar horrors. Professor Kipnis brings social, psychological, cultural, and dramatic insight into the effects of this perversion of a legitimate law. The effect of this "politically correct" Title IX expansion on academic freedom is also well documented in Robert Shibley's book *Twisting Title IX*, summarizing his Foundation for Individual Rights in Education's (FIRE) which champions advocacy of freedom of speech. He points out that the gender discrimination prohibited by Title IX is deftly extended to include sexual harassment and "misconduct," including "verbal and nonverbal," which anyone does not like or by which anyone is offended. So, any remark, gesture, joke, facial expression, appearance, or opinion that upsets anyone (especially in "protected" groups) can violate the University Title IX policy.[10] An "offender" is then investigated, interrogated

---

[10] Robert L. Shibley, *Twisting Title IX* (New York: Encounter Books, 2016) 24–25. A group of Harvard Law School faculty immediately saw the ramifications of this expansion in 2014 and wrote an open letter, published in *The Boston Globe* famously saying it is "inconsistent with many of the most basic principles we teach."

(without the benefits of the due process of law normally afforded the accused), and judged (expelled, reprimanded, fired, etc.) by a single Title IX official beholden to a Washington agency with power over the university, the Constitution, the federal judiciary, and Congress. Well, the Federal Courts did not agree with that for very long.

Besides the destruction of freedom of speech, necessary to a healthy university education, this Title IX policy and its procedures create an atmosphere of suspicion, fear, and persecution, inimical to an open, free, and happy academic community. The offended are encouraged by university Title IX offices, with Orwellian names like The Office of Conduct and Compliance, to report any infraction of these totalitarian codes, against themselves or others, to launch an inquisition and seek persecution and punishment. Spying, surveillance, and reporting any possibly infringement (on- or off-campus, anytime of the year, for perpetuity) create a police-state environment not seen since the Nazi Gestapo of Germany in the 1930s. Obviously this creates a "hostile environment" for everyone by turning lively, exciting, challenging, and pleasant universities into cold, hostile, and fearful graveyards.

## Rolling Stone Magazine Article and UVa

Sadly, one of the most notorious Title IX tragedies occurred at Mr. Jefferson's citadel of academic freedom: The University of Virginia. The infamous "Rolling Stone Magazine Episode" showed the extent of the destruction of these policies to reason, intellectual activity, and healthy academic communities.

By the fall of 2014, the government's expansion and publicity of Title IX led a majority of Americans to believe that universities were centers of massive violence and oppression—that many people at U.S. institutions of higher education were continually being assaulted, abused, and harassed. This crisis justified the draconian policies that policed "conduct" of faculty, staff, and students. The problem was particularly framed in terms of white men assaulting, abusing and harassing minorities and women.

In this atmosphere, the most publicized atrocity of the kind was reported by *Rolling Stone Magazine*. In November of 2014, this magazine's cover story was of a horrific rape at The University of Virginia, in a fraternity house. National media attention and outrage in Charlottesville followed. The incident seemed to confirm all the Title IX advocates asserted about the "culture of rape" at American universities—their "toxic masculinity" and fraternity brutality. The UVa Administration temporarily suspended all fraternities and sororities. The accused fraternity house was vandalized—windows were broken by bricks and bottles thrown by protestors, and fraternity members were attacked on campus and in social media. But, as the facts in this case were investigated by law enforcement officials and other journalists, it was found to be entirely fabricated by the false accuser. But the story and the institutional response greatly damaged the University of Virginia's reputation: applications were down, as were benefactions and rankings.

The UVa Board of Visitors subsequently hired an international team of law firms to investigate how the Administration had handled this crisis.

In April of 2017, *Rolling Stone Magazine* settled a three-million-dollar lawsuit against a dean, defamed in the article, and in June, 2017, 1.65-million-dollar lawsuit was settled with the libeled fraternity.

In July, 2017, UVa implemented a revised Title IX policy that restored many constitutional protections to freedom of speech and due process of law.

Also, in its 2017 term, the United States Supreme Court ruled in a First Amendment's freedom-of-speech case (Matal v. Tam) that the government cannot restrict speech on the basis of it offending an individual's or a group's "identity." In a unanimous decision by the Court, it stated, "Speech may not be banned on the ground that it expresses ideas that offend." This ruling should end the "politically correct" speech codes, restrictions ("verbal harassment"), and policies of Title IX, damaging academic freedom.

Even the new administration in Washington seems to be revising the recent Title IX policy expansion. Secretary of Education, De Vos, said of it: "There are some things that are working. There are many things that are not working well."[11] On September 22, 2017, the U.S. Department of Education Office of Civil Rights rescinded the 2011 and 2014 expansions of Title IX.

But in November, 2016, a group of UVA faculty and students petitioned the President of the University to stop quoting Jefferson because he owned slaves and was a racist. Mr. Jefferson's ideal of rational, free speech in the academy had reached a new low.

In November, 2015, the Faculty Senate of The University of Virginia's College at Wise unanimously adopted a Resolution on Academic Freedom, which I crafted. There is an addendum, "Reasons for Academic Freedom," which details the philosophical, historical, and social benefits of Jeffersonian academia—a subject of national publicity which affects other universities—for a thriving educational experience.[12] The Jeffersonian liberal values of justice, freedom, moral sensitivity, and worthwhile industry must prevail at all colleges and universities. With his usual optimism, Jefferson believed that as long as humans have reason and a social nature, the intellectual life of the university will prevail.

---

[11] *Inside Higher Ed,* July 14, 2017.
[12] "Virginia Professors Adopt Statement Championing Academic Freedom, Free Speech," *The College Fix* (site) January 5, 2016.

# Book Reviews

*The Key to the Door: Experiences of Early African American Students at the University of Virginia.* Maurice Apprey and Shelli M. Poe (Charlottesville: University of Virginia Press, 2017).

Reviewed by **M. Andrew Holowchak, Ph.D.**, Editor, *The Journal of Thomas Jefferson's Life and Times,* Philosophy, University of Colorado, Colorado Springs

Apprey and Poe's *The Key to the Door*, an account of the stories of "seven of the University's pioneering African American students," is a book about opening the door to equality of opportunity at UVa. These are stories of courage and fear, persistency through felt failure, and triumph through endurance or through determination. I includes some snippets.

John Merchant expresses the fear he continually experienced as he was the first Black that graduated from the University. "My arrival," says Merchant, "marked the beginning of a three-year experience during which I cannot recall being unafraid for any extended period of time." He got through the experience with the prodding of his father and a little shared bourbon with one of the UVa professors on a special occasion.

William Womack, remarkable successful throughout his early education, came to UVa to earn a medical degree but was put off by expectations that he, on account of his color, would fail. During a psychiatry clerkship at UVa, the chair of Psychiatry convinced Womack to take up psychiatry and suggested matriculation at University of Washington. Womack did just that, and wound up as the first Black professor in the Department of Psychiatry at Washington.

Aubrey Jones, accepted into the UVa's School of Engineering, recalls the cumbersome pressure to succeed. "It was as though we had the weight of the black community on our shoulders. If we failed, we felt that it would not only be a bad reflection on ourselves but it might keep other blacks from attending U.V.a." Moreover, failure would confirm many Whites' suspicions that Blacks did not belong at a top-tier institution. Jones survived through rigorous studying and "an extended family at U.V.a."—custodians, cooks, and maintenance personnel who did what they could, behind the scenes, as it were, to assist.

Barbara Favazza began medical school at UVa in 1962. She recalled no racist treatment by professors. Yet she too felt the weighty pressure of "representing a whole group of people." She received her degree in 1966.

David Temple, Jr., a political activist during his youth, talks about the significance of personages such as Martin Luther King and John F. Kennedy in shaping his character. The famous words of Kennedy, asking for public service and not political hand-outs, resonated with him. "I breathed and absorbed every word. From that moment to this day, public service would define and drive me." He earned a bachelor's in Psychology in 1969 at UVa, returned in 1971 to work on and earn a master's in Special Education, and continued his non-violent activism concerning racial equality during his tenure at UVa.

William McLeod, a *soi-disant* "trailblazer," writes of the persistency and encouragement of his mother, Hattie Lee, who would work in the fields and pick 300 pounds of cotton each day so William could go to school and have a better life. In 1964, McLeod graduated from Fayettesville State University and went to the Curry School of Education at UVa to earn a master's. "It was at that time that I developed my passion for educational leadership."

Finally, Vivian Pinn, in an interview by Apprey, talks of her experiences as being only the second black female in the Medical School. For Pinn, the smallest things were of great consequence. In a class on anatomy, for illustration, her professor asked students to arrange themselves in groups of four. Each group was to comprise one's anatomy partners for the year. Sensing that no one would pick her, she felt panicky till two classmates approached her and said, "We'd like for you to be our lab partner." She endured the process through her family, especially her father, and the Charlottesville black community.

When we read such stories, we are moved first by the unrelenting courage of such students in the face of obstacles. It is one thing to be driven to succeed because of the rewards, internal and otherwise, of that success. It is quite another thing to be driven to succeed because failure will likely retard movement toward racial justice, because failure will reinforce inveterate racism. That is quite a burden to place on young shoulders.

Moreover, we are also moved by the stories behind the stories—viz., the people behind the scenes at or around UVa who helped to make the institution what it is today. There were slaves at UVa, such as slave Lewis Commodore, who became the university's bell-ringer, and the bell was to be rung at dawn, prior to each of the three meals, and before classes. There were black employees, who helped black students insofar as they saw in them the hope for a more just tomorrow. There were the parents and friends of the students who egged them on to success through words of encouragement or through offering a place to repast and unwind. There was the black community of Charlottesville that proved helpful to some, like Merchant and Pinn. Finally, there were many in the white community of students and professors who did what they could to ensure the success of black students.

Highly recommended reading. Kudos to Apprey and Poe for putting together such a collection of intriguing essays.

---

***The Virginia Presidents: A Travel and History Guide.*** Richard E. Dixon (Clifton Books, 2014)

Reviewed by **M. Andrew Holowchak**, Editor, *The Journal of the Life and Times of Thomas Jefferson*

There were eight presidents from Virginia—the first being George Washington and the last being Woodrow Wilson—and four of the first five presidents were Virginians, each holding the first office for two terms. That is an astonishing contribution to the founding, development, and governance of the United States over the years. The author of this useful guidebook, Richard Dixon, a native of Virginia, is clearly proud of that contribution to the nation. *The Virginia Presidents* is a testament to that pride.

"The purpose of this book is to provide the reader with the historical context of the presidential sites," writes Dixon at the end of his introduction. The book, nearly 200 pages in length, comprises a brief history of the forming of the nation in two short chapters before it segues into chapters on each of the Virginian presidents: Washington, Jefferson, Madison, Monroe, Harrison, Tyler, Taylor, and Wilson.

Each short chapter is composed of a brief history of each president with numerous text-boxes with information concerning historically relevant landmarks such as Historic Jamestowne, Washington's Grist Mill and Distillery, the Natural Bridge, Hollywood Cemetery, and Tyler's Sherwood Forest Plantation; historically significant persons such as John Marshall, George Mason, Tecumseh, and Dolley Payne Madison; historically relevant incidents; and historically relevant tidbits such as the story of Mount Vernon, a text-box on slavery, and an account of the first Thanksgiving; among other things. Historically relevant landmarks have information relevant to persons wishing to visit under the labels "Visitors," "Directions," and "Contact." The first tells when a landmark can be visited and if there are guided tours and a gift shop. The second is self-evident. The last lists addresses, relevant phone numbers, and web-pages.

The work is not meant to be read cover to cover. Doing so will disappoint a reader. It is, after all, a guide book, not a history book. It is meant to be read in small doses—perhaps prior to or just after a visit to, say, Monticello or the Woodrow Wilson Presidential Library and Museum. That said, there is more than enough history in the guidebook to inform plentifully uninformed readers.

Readers wishing for more information are rewarded with six appendices. The first two offer short biographies of the vice-presidents and wives of the Virginian presidents. The third offers useful advice for anyone planning a trip to Virginia. Appendix 4 gives a map of Virginia, which unfortunately is neither complete nor clear, but it does give an aidful website to accompany the picture. The fifth appendix offers information for further reading. The final appendix cites merely cites the sources of the pictures, included in the book.

Thus, if you are planning a visit to any of the sites that help to tell the story of any of the Virginian presidents, Dixon's guidebook is not just recommended reading, it is a required travelling companion.

# Letter to the Editor

Dear Editor:

I found Professor Ari Helo's article, *Jefferson's Progressive View of History Revisiting the Ludlow Letter,* very illuminating. Professor Helo not only provided further insight into the mind of Thomas Jefferson, but also laid out for us a stark contrast between Jefferson's understanding of progressivism, and progressivism as it has been understood since the dawn of the modern-day Progressive Era (1880s) in American politics.

Jefferson's understanding of progressivism was of course rooted in the 18th century Enlightenment—the Age of Reason. Although the Enlightenment was a highly varied, multi-faceted, and complex historical era, its constant theme focused on structured, scientific-based thinking, and an insatiable quest for new knowledge. The collective aim of the movers and shakers of the Enlightenment focused on making the human condition significantly better.

Thomas Jefferson was greatly influenced by the people in his life who introduced him to the Enlightenment: William Small and George Wythe of the College of William and Mary, several French *philosophes* with whom he associated in the salons of Paris during his time in France (1784-1789), and others. Thomas Jefferson was also a person of letters and a person of books. Many of his correspondences helped shape his progressive views, people such as John and Abigail Adams, David Rittenhouse, the Marquis de Chastellux, and Benjamin Banneker. Through constant reading—"I cannot live without books," he once wrote to John Adams—Jefferson became influenced by many of the great thinkers from antiquity to his era, touching upon intellectual pursuits ranging from history to medicine, philosophy, mathematics, the natural and physical sciences, and so forth.

Perhaps in no other intellectual realm in which Jefferson invested considerable time in splendid contemplation and articulation were the fruits of his progressive thinking more profound than in the area of political theory. There Jefferson's education (formal and informal) and ideas converged and blossomed at a then historically unprecedented level. As Professor Helo emphasized, Jefferson for sure anticipated continual moral and intellectual progress among humankind. Yet Jefferson was no utopian, as Professor Helo also correctly concluded. Ultimately, Jefferson rejected utopianism, primarily because of his acceptance of the idea that human beings were capable of producing both the good and bad. Indeed, that has been the state of the human condition throughout the ages, Jefferson apparently reasoned. Moreover, based on the corpus of his political writings, Jefferson also believed that government, a reflection of the human condition, was likewise capable of both the good and bad, but never capable of utopian perfection.

Since the dawn of the so-called Progressive Era in American politics, American-style Progressivism has been based on an underlying assumption that the forces of evolution are forever moving humanity toward intellectual and moral perfection, with government moving along the same trajectory in the process. Modern Progressivism also emphasizes that an elite class of enlightened and well-educated sages can govern humanity justly. Those Progressive views are the complete antithesis of the progressive views held and advanced by the Sage of Monticello—at very least they are in significant conflict with one another. In the former model, an elite have the duty and right to rule. In the Jefferson model, the people are sovereign. Thus the two views of progressivism are fundamentally not the same.

Perhaps that great intellectual chasm is best observed through a statement once made by Woodrow Wilson, an earlier leading proponent of Progressivism. In response to the preamble to the Declaration of Independence, Wilson had this to say in an address he made to the Jefferson Club in Los Angeles, California, in 1911. He said, "If you want to understand the real Declaration of Independence, do not repeat the preface [preamble]." Wilson thus rejected the notion that our liberties stem from natural rights coming from God. Also, in his protest, Wilson reduced the Declaration of Independence to an anachronistic 18th century document that merely contained a list of grievances against a now long dead potentate. Mr. Jefferson undoubtedly would have protested that Wilsonian view.

Dave Dietrich
Forest, VA

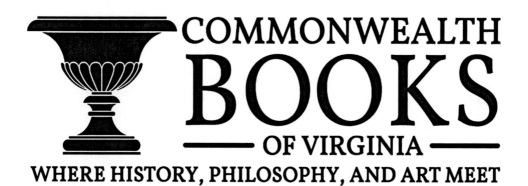

# COMMONWEALTH BOOKS OF VIRGINIA
## WHERE HISTORY, PHILOSOPHY, AND ART MEET

Commonwealth Books of Virginia publishes historical commentaries, non-fiction narratives in History and Political Philosophy, memoirs, historical fiction, and pictorial narrative.

We produce beautiful books, which we promote into all channels of the book trade. Our readers expect to expand their horizons while enjoying themselves. If you have a manuscript that fits this profile, send us information about it at: www.commonwealthbooks.org/pages/submissions, or contact us at: info@commonwealthbooks.org.

Commonwealth Books of Virginia | Richmond, Virginia | 703-307-7715
www.commonwealthbooks.org

---

## THOMAS JEFFERSON'S ENLIGHTENMENT – PARIS 1785: A Pictorial Narrative

See what Jefferson saw while perusing 168 museum-quality reproductions of painting, portraits, prints, and period maps. Become enlightened as Jefferson did as Pierre Cabanis guides "the savage from the mountains of America" through the capital of the most elegant—and debauched—society in the world.

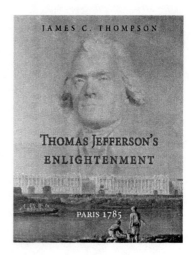

Cloth Edition: $45.00
ISBN: 978-0-9854863-1-0
Color: 9.25 x 12.25
Pages: 166
Images: 168

Paperback Edition: $28.00
ISBN: 978-0-9854863-9-6
Color: 8.5 x 11.0
Pages: 166
Images: 168

Online at: www.commonwealthbooks.org/collections/all/products/thomas-jefferson-s-enlightenment-paris-1785-illustrated-edition.

CPSIA information can be obtained
at www.ICGtesting.com
Printed in the USA
FFOW05n1632201117